'I read this moving and honest testimony in one sitting. Amanda writes in a very frank way which I found drew me in and made me want to keep reading! I recommend it to anyone who has experienced or is concerned about how challenging relationships can affect us right into adulthood. Through her many pains and difficulties we see God at work drawing Amanda into a wonderful relationship with Himself and leading her into a life of fruitful and joyful service for Him. The story of Amanda and her brother Andrew raises important issues around justice and mental health and again and again reveals the loving Father Heart of God, especially towards those who have been most wounded and alienated. What a great testimony it is to God's grace.'
Celia Bowring, Operations Director at CARE

'Mandy's story is both tragic and inspiring. She's overcome neglect, abuse and trauma to build a life of faith that we can all learn from. This book is well worth a read.'
Amaris Cole, Editor, Evangelical Alliance

D1335260

Coming Home to Dad

A journey from childhood trauma to wholeness

Amanda Pilz

instant
ap⬚stle

First published in Great Britain in 2016

Instant Apostle
The Barn
1 Watford House Lane
Watford
Herts
WD17 1BJ

Copyright © Amanda Pilz 2016

British Library Cataloguing-in-Publication Data

A catalogue record for this book is available from the British Library.

This book and all other Instant Apostle books are available from Instant Apostle:
Website: www.instantapostle.com
E-mail: info@instantapostle.com

ISBN 978-1-909728-55-4

Printed in Great Britain

Instant Apostle is a pioneering publishing house that exists to inspire followers of Jesus and promote the values of His Kingdom in the world.

Instant Apostle was founded to publish books by writers who are passionate about addressing diverse social issues from a Kingdom perspective – in any and every genre. Whether it is faith-building autobiography, riveting fiction, engaging study in Christian mindfulness or compassionate response to mental health problems, if a book is well written, original and authentic you will find it with us. We want to share Kingdom values with everyone, and publish titles that cross into secular markets, particularly in adults' and children's fiction.

Instant Apostle books engage with varied and poignant subjects, from child sex-trafficking and autism to the plight of asylum seekers and the challenges of young people growing up in the social media age. These are books by informed, creative and sometimes opinionated people that demolish stale paradigms and foster faith in Jesus.

Working with established writers and actively welcoming new authors, Instant Apostle seeks out prophetic voices that will change the way readers young and old understand God's Kingdom and see the world! Are you ready to join us?

Share the passion. Get reading. Get writing. Get published!

To Mum, Andrew, Tristan and Zack,
and to the fatherless

'A father to the fatherless'
(Psalm 68:5)

Acknowledgements

I had never planned to write a book, certainly not an autobiographical one. However, it was during a telephone conversation with Manoj Raithatha of Instant Apostle that the seed for this book was sown. Manoj, you are a godly risk taker.

Thanks go to Amaris Cole, editor of *idea* magazine at the Evangelical Alliance who, shortly after, unwittingly watered that seed by suggesting I write about my childhood experiences.

A big thank you to my surrogate dad, David Gould who, from his home in Canada, spent many hours editing the first wordy draft. Your commitment to concision in writing is a lesson for me.

I want to thank the team at Instant Apostle and Sheila Jacobs, a wonderful editor, who not only patiently scrutinised and edited the manuscript, but also engaged with the book's content and encouraged me greatly.

Gratitude also goes to Beverley Hymers, my long-time true friend, who read through the chapters and gave helpful feedback and to trusty friend, Joyce Ng-Setlhare, who helped to track down Marion in Botswana.

Finally, all thanks and praise go to my heavenly Father. This is Your story.

Contents

Chapter 1
Early childhood

The bedroom door suddenly flew open. I blinked as the hallway light flooded the darkness. A stout silhouette stood in the doorway and, before I had time to react, the figure strode over to me and I felt a hot, searing pain just to the left of the top of my head as I was hauled from the bed by my hair. I could feel my heart racing as, still in a tight grip, I was dragged from the ground-floor bedroom, through the kitchen and the dining area and into the connecting lounge, to where Dad was quietly sitting in an armchair by the fire.

'Say goodnight to ya' father!' my captor demanded, still maintaining her grip.

Trembling in my nightdress and finally released, I cautiously approached Dad and kissed his smooth cheek while he sat, motionless and silent. Then I turned and fled back to bed, giving vent to my anguish in hot tears.

My dad is called Robert, Rob for short, but I have little idea about who he really is. My early memories of him are few, the main image being that of a man sitting in our back room listening to the radio drama *Waggoner's Walk*, shrouded in a cloud of smoke emanating either from his pipe or from working his way through a packet of cigarettes. Dad often went through 40 cigarettes a day, and no one thought twice about the fact that children were breathing in the smoke.

He had been adopted as a one-month-old baby, raised as an only child and had left school at age 15. His first job was driving a van, delivering televisions for an electrical firm. It hadn't seemed a very promising start but he wasn't afraid of hard work and was determined to make something of himself. This, to him, was synonymous with making as much money as possible. Consequently it wasn't long before he 'graduated' from driving a van to working as a bailiff, arriving with a burly henchman on debtors' doorsteps. From there he took a job with a finance firm in Beverley, and began working his way up through company promotions. Dad was a workaholic, with family coming very much second.

He was born in Hull in 1934, the eighth child of a family in that city. His father was a professional violinist who played in the Hull Orchestra, but beyond that nothing is known of the family, not even their name. Dad never wanted to know the identity of his real parents. The story goes that it was because of financial hardship that he was given away for adoption, a fact which appeared to have left him hard and embittered. However, his adoptive parents, Elsie and Edward Webster, who lived in Hull and later Hornsea, a small and little known seaside town in East Yorkshire, provided him with a loving home, and it was in Hornsea that he spent his entire childhood.

He met Ann, my mum, at Hornsea Congregational Church, as it was then known, where he was the organist and she attended Sunday services. He was 23; she was 17. Her parents were not churchgoers but Mum liked to attend worship because it helped to ease her anxiety and depression. She played the piano and was interested in learning how to work a pipe organ, so Dad offered to teach her. At the time she was studying shorthand typing and bookkeeping at college, and later took a job as a shorthand typist.

Mum was strikingly attractive. Relatively tall for a woman, she had a slim, shapely figure, thick blonde hair, fair skin, blue eyes and regular, aquiline features. She and her brother David, who had thick, curly, dark hair, were both exceptionally good-looking.

Dad, however, was not especially tall for a man. He had swarthy-looking, rather oily skin, greenish eyes and jet black hair with a significant bald patch for a man in his twenties. He kept one side of his hair quite long, scraping it over the top of his head in an attempt to disguise the hair loss. This rarely achieved the desired result as it only took a small puff of wind for the long strands to be blown out of place and left hanging to his shoulder, creating an odd look. Unlike Mum, his face and features were rather rounded – his nose a little bulbous and his teeth small and crowded.

Needless to say, Dad wasted no time in pursuing Mum and made a habit of waiting outside her workplace to give her a lift home. Her employer, somewhat concerned about whether Dad's attentions were welcome, sought to keep Dad at bay by occasionally offering her a lift himself. In the end, given that there wasn't much choice of marriage partners in Hornsea, Mum, somewhat hesitantly, went along with the relationship.

Dad's interest in her was also not welcomed by Mum's parents, Fred and Kathleen Stephenson. They disliked him, thinking him devious and unsuitable. They tried to keep him at a distance, but to no avail.

Then the bombshell dropped. Mum was pregnant. It was unplanned. Dad said he would go ahead and marry her. It was the honourable thing to do, even in the early 1960s when people, possibly in response to the war experience, were actively throwing off the constraints of the past. However, Fred had other ideas and told Dad that he and Kathleen would help to raise the child and that marriage wouldn't be necessary.

But Dad was determined and wouldn't take no for an answer. So in the course of time, a shotgun wedding took place on 27 January 1962 when Mum, aged 21, was three months pregnant. The wedding was attended by both sets of parents, very much aware of the unfortunate circumstances surrounding it.

My brother, Andrew, was duly born in July 1962, and I arrived on the scene in the thick of winter in December 1964. Deep snow covered the ground as Dad set off for Bridlington District Hospital where Mum was having difficulty pushing me out. Thanks to the hospital staff giving her a dose of cod liver oil (or so it was believed), I entered the world covered in faeces. After being bathed I was presented to Mum: pink, clean and with my shock of jet-black hair protruding from the cream-coloured baby shawl I was wrapped in. I was to be christened Amanda Webster, taking Dad's adoptive family name.

I was considered to be a big baby at 8lb 5oz, and Mum came to refer to me as a 'bouncing rubber ball' as my cheeks formed dimples and I grew into a chubby, robust baby.

We lived in Hornsea during the first few years of my life. When I was a toddler Mum would take my brother to and from school, pushing me along in a stroller on a rough dirt track which traversed a piece of waste ground. While she rushed along I liked to lean over and stare at the rough, stony ground which seemed to form patterns as it flashed by.

Dad wasn't especially hands-on with us when we were small children, much preferring to sit comfortably, observing us from a distance as we played. But now and then he would put me on his shoulders and I, giggling mischievously, would place my hands over his glasses to prevent him seeing where he was going. I felt happy in my toddler world, blissfully unaware of any growing unease within the family about my parents' increasingly strained relationship.

When I was four, Dad had to relocate because of his work and we moved to Marton-in-Cleveland, near Middlesborough. Dad appeared to work very long hours, arriving home well after my brother and I had been put to bed and leaving for work before we were woken up for school, so we spent little time with him. Many years later I learned it was during this period that he infected Mum with gonorrhoea. The reason for his late nights at the office then became clear. Dad himself had to wear a bandage round his private parts until the infection cleared up.

We lived in an unremarkable semi-detached three-bedroomed house. It had two reception rooms, one at the front and another at the back, the back one being connected to the kitchen by a serving hatch through which food could conveniently be passed. The equally ordinary first floor consisted of two medium-sized bedrooms, a small bathroom, a separate toilet and a small box room at the front – the room that became mine for a while. We had two cars – one for Mum and the other for Dad, each one a Hillman Minx.

When I wasn't at school I would play with my brother in our back garden or with the girl next door, who had a swing and climbing equipment, unlike our own less exciting garden which only contained an inflatable paddling pool during summer. We often played out in the street, fighting in rival 'gangs': my brother and I and the children next door versus the siblings on the road perpendicular to ours. This 'warfare' consisted of a lot of shouting, running and throwing of stones. We often ventured further afield, unaccompanied by adults, to a swampy, wooded area with a 'haunted' ruin of a house, to play freely, returning home in the early evening. Mindful of the 'bogeyman', a scare tactic of adult warnings to not talk to strangers, we were always on the lookout for this mythical figure who, in my mind, would be identified as a grey-looking old man with straggly hair and beard, a wide-brimmed hat and a long, shabby raincoat.

Being the younger child I often coveted my brother's more advanced toys. I felt my tricycle was no match for his go-kart and blue bicycle, especially as my tricycle had a large, cumbersome tin box attached to the back for carrying things. Every time I turned my tricycle round in the passage which ran between our garage and that of our neighbour, the box scraped against the passage's brick walls, causing an ugly rust spot to form on one of its corners. Wanting to progress to a two-wheeler, I made it my goal to climb onto my brother's bike as often as possible and teach myself to ride it.

Dad continued to be a relatively distant figure in our lives at this time, and the memories of him are few. But a couple stand out: I was in the kitchen, feeling frightened because he was shouting at Mum. He angrily hurled a pan across the room into the sink, where it landed with an ear-splitting crash. Another was the moment he walked through the front door with a very large teddy bear for me, golden-yellow in colour, and wrapped in a cellophane bag. The bear was a relatively rare show of affection, which could be why this memory remains with me to this day. It told me that somehow Dad did care.

I also felt I was Dad's favourite. He often called me 'little one', and I experienced a warmth, a good feeling of being approved of. I felt that he loved me even if he never actually said so.

Dad was quite an accomplished organist, even stretching to *Widor's Toccata and Fugue*, a complex classical organ piece. Most Sundays during my early years Mum, Dad, my brother and I would go as a family to St John's, a big, dark and imposing Anglican church in Middlesborough. Andrew would sometimes sing in the choir while Dad led the hymns on the enormous pipe organ. In my early years I grew up listening to the sound of its powerful strains.

25

The inside of the church was quite dark and cavernous as well as cold, with creaking wooden pews which always smelled of polish. It wasn't a family-friendly church, and if I or my brother made too much noise, Mum would be asked to take us out. It seemed church was a place for adults in serious and quiet reflection; it wasn't a place for children, and squeals from excited youngsters climbing over the pews were most unwelcome.

The vicar of this church was one of Dad's few friends and would call round to our house on occasion to sit and drink tea. However, faith itself, at least as far as Dad was concerned, didn't appear to be the primary reason for this church connection. For Mum, however, it was continuing a habit she had started in her teens, although I don't know how much she understood at this time because Christian belief was never discussed in our family. In spite of that, Andrew and I were taken to Sunday school somewhere near our home on the days when we didn't go to St John's. I speculate it was here that I first heard the words 'Jesus died for you', which became lodged in my memory throughout my childhood. However, I didn't understand their significance, nor did I make any connection between Christianity and my own behaviour.

One day at the local newsagent's, I stood eyeing the shelves of sweets which had been neatly arranged at a height suitable for children. My coat pockets were wide and my right hand was just inches from a row of fruit pastilles. It would be so easy to slip a packet unnoticed into my pocket – so I did. Instinctively I knew immediately that this was wrong, and when I arrived home the fear of being discovered propelled me straight into the lounge where I hid behind the sofa in the semi-dark. Wanting to destroy the evidence of my wrongdoing, I quickly stuffed the sweets one after the other into my mouth until the packet was finished. I had got away with it.

Life went on in this way until one day something happened which was to dramatically change our family. Mum told me she was going away for a while. Dad had said he thought she needed a break – that she should go to my grandmother's in Scarborough for a week or two.

'Go to your mother's for a break, Ann,' he had told her.

She packed enough clothes for two weeks – but I felt troubled. 'I don't want you to go,' I pleaded with her as, with lights out, she tucked me up for the night in my little box room.

'I haven't gone yet,' she replied breezily, as if there were nothing to worry about. But my six-year-old mind told me otherwise. Something wasn't right.

Chapter 2
Separation

I have no memory of Mum's going, yet I had a sense that she might not be back as soon as I had hoped. This was made clearer the day after she left when the front door to our house swung open and an unfamiliar woman strode in. I was standing, naked, on the stairs, on my way to have a bath, when she approached and invited me to take a biscuit from a large tin she was holding. I had no idea what she was doing in our home.

Unknown to me, two weeks after Mum left, a letter arrived for her at my grandmother's house. It was from Dad, saying, 'There's no need for you to come back. I've got someone else in.'

This sudden change in our family was the beginning of deep unhappiness in my and Andrew's lives. No one sat down with us to explain these new arrangements. Separated from our mother and placed into the hands of a stranger, we were simply expected to accept these arrangements and continue with our lives as if nothing had happened. Dad's presence in our daily routine diminished even more as the newcomer took over, and our days consisted mostly of going to school and playing outside.

This neat set-up suited Dad and the woman who was now, to all intents and purposes, our stepmother. However, as far as Andrew and I were concerned, our lives, which had been reasonably happy, were now plunged into darkness as we tried to navigate the new situation we found ourselves in. We wanted to escape and return to Mum who, as far as we knew, now had little choice but to live 50 miles away with her parents in Scarborough.

Feeling helpless, Andrew and I developed a habit of standing at his bedroom window looking down on to the street and up at the sky which, in the evening, was veiled by an orange smog accompanied by a sweet, chemical smell from Middlesborough's industrial areas. This ritual was our way of expressing a longing for Mum, a longing to leave. But the scene through the window was of an adult world which we could not navigate. We talked about running away and catching a bus to find her, but we knew it was impossible because we had no money or any idea about local public transport. So instead we often fantasised about escaping, making each other giggle with endless examples of how Mum would rescue us.

'Imagine if she came to rescue us rolling on an egg or riding on a piece of toast,' we would say.

My stepmother's name was Ella. I was too young to take in much about her, but my brother and I were clearly so unhappy that we were taken to a child psychologist to find out why. I remember sitting in front of her being asked to fit different shaped blocks into their correct holes. I didn't understand why I had to do this and was worried about getting the exercise wrong – that I might fail the 'test'.

Following the psychologist's assessment, Andrew and I were prescribed an antidepressant. Looking back, the question seemed to be, 'What is wrong with these children?' rather than, 'What is wrong with the circumstances they are in?'

In the early days with Ella, Andrew and I developed a ritual called 'the seek', so named because it was our secret. Once lights were out we would leave our respective bedrooms and meet on the landing in the dark; Andrew in his pyjamas and I in my nightdress. We would sit on the floor, facing one another, and press the soles of our feet together, then reach forward and clasp one another's hands. Then we began to rock back and forth, sometimes trying to pull each other hard enough to be lifted off the ground and land with a bump while giggling hysterically at the silliness and secrecy of it. 'The seek' bound us together and was comforting, helping us to feel less alone. The rocking and giggling served as an outlet from the troubled circumstances in which we found ourselves. Because I shared 'the seek' with Andrew and no one else, it was somehow empowering. It would only end when we heard the padding of Ella's footsteps coming upstairs to see what we were doing, at which point we would dart at lightning speed back to our beds.

Then, in the middle of this unhappiness, something happened that caused huge excitement and hope to dawn in our hearts.

'Your mum's here for you,' my teacher announced one day as I sat in class. Surprised, as I thought Mum was in Scarborough, I stood up and collected my coat before being led out of the classroom and to the main entrance of

Captain Cook's Junior School. The sight of Mum thrilled me, as did the fact that I was to join my brother, my grandmother (whom my brother and I, through a series of rhymes and word associations, had affectionately nicknamed 'Span') and my grandfather, 'Gramps', for a ride in a large black taxi. As soon as we had jumped inside, the door slammed shut and we were off, the driver confidently steering as we sped along, winding this way and that, swiftly making our way through the suburban streets.

Stopping outside our house we all scrambled out, except for Andrew, and Gramps took the lead as we walked up the path to the front door. I sensed a drama unfolding and was filled with excitement and fear. I was about to face my stepmother under hostile circumstances.

Ella came to the door, and no sooner had she opened it than Gramps threw his full weight against it, forcing his way past her into the entrance. We all piled in behind him. In desperation, Ella reached for the house phone which was positioned on a nearby table, but Gramps immediately tore the telephone wire away from the wall and smashed the receiver across his knee, breaking it into two pieces. I looked on wide-eyed. Meanwhile, Mum rushed up the stairs with a large suitcase to retrieve her clothes. I, seeing an opportunity, picked up my brother's football boot, which was lying in the hallway, and repeatedly hammered it as hard as I could against Ella's chunky thigh, noticing as I did so that she was wearing an expensive pencil skirt made from silky, pink material. The presence of adults who I knew were on my side gave me courage, and I relished the opportunity to hit a woman I had come to hate.

I wanted her to know what I thought of her. I wanted to pay her back because, as I saw it, she had destroyed our family.

After collecting Mum's clothes and some of mine and Andrew's, we left a dazed Ella and scrambled back into the taxi to set out on the return journey across the wild and desolate North York Moors. But as we were crossing this area, the taxi broke down.

'I *knew* we should have used a newer car,' lamented Span.

How on earth would we make good our escape now? We knew it wouldn't be long before Dad would be on this very road in hot pursuit. Thankfully, the taxi driver had the necessary skills to get the engine started again and we were able to continue our journey. The 'raid' had succeeded and we soon arrived safely at Span and Gramps' two-bedroomed bungalow on the elevated coastal outskirts of Scarborough.

That evening, knowing Dad would soon be on Span's doorstep, we were on our guard, doors locked and windows closed. Hearing a loud banging on the front door, I peeped through the tiny porch of the bungalow. I could see a familiar fawn-coloured cardigan on the other side of the opaque glass of the front door. Dad was standing there, knocking.

Like two trapped animals, my brother and I tore at top speed back through the lounge. Andrew, ahead of me, shot into the tiny bathroom, locking the door behind him. 'Let me in,' I urged him through the closed door, tugging at the handle and pushing futilely against the locked door.

'Go and find your own hiding place,' he hissed back.

I couldn't believe it. My brother, who had shared in all the turmoil, was now abandoning me. Didn't he care that I might be taken away? I turned and shot into Span's bedroom, launched myself over one of the beds and squeezed myself into the narrow space between it and the wall. I lay there in the semi-darkness, my heart racing, waiting for something terrible to happen.

It didn't. On this occasion Dad failed to capture us – but we knew it was far from over. That night my brother and I slept on camp beds squashed into my grandmother's bedroom, with Mum and Span in beds on either side, while Gramps slept in the other smaller bedroom. The whole episode had been so traumatic and frightening that once in bed, I emptied my bowels on the sheets – much to Gramps' anger.

The next day Andrew and I were woken early and taken into Scarborough town centre by Span while Mum kept a lookout for Dad at the bungalow. The plan was for us to spend the day hiding in some leafy gardens on St Nicholas Cliff. The gardens had numerous winding paths which led all the way down to the seafront. We aimed to stay here until Dad gave up the chase and went home. Feeling bored after spending so long in the gardens, we eventually made our way down the paths to the beach front. Somehow Mum located us as we stood at the bottom of the McBean Steps, which, parallel to the gardens, led down the cliff to the seafront. She appeared at the top of the steps and shouted the warning, 'Rob's in town!'

It was no good, of course. Several days later Andrew and I found ourselves on the back seat of Dad's metallic blue Ford Zephyr journeying back to Marton.

'He's got custard,' we anxiously reminded one another – our word for 'custody' – the word which kept us from being with the person we most wanted: Mum. The hope that we might finally have escaped from our unhappy world with Ella had been dashed to pieces. The darkness returned, and with every mile that Dad's car covered came a growing sense of dread.

On our return from Span's after the 'raid', our lives were expected to carry on as though there had been no interruption. There appeared to be no light and no prospect of any change for the better.

Then, one day, I was sitting in the front room watching television when a girl of similar age to me, around eight years old, appeared on the screen. She was being interviewed and mentioned that she had 'met God'. My attention was momentarily arrested. I was struck by her words. They only lasted a matter of seconds, but I was intrigued. There and then I decided that I would like to meet God too. It seemed to tap straight into a notion I had had from a very young age, the origin of which was unknown to me, that one day something very special was going to happen to me. I didn't know what it was or when it would happen. It was an intuitive thought that I carried around with me, and I enjoyed the mystery and anticipation of it.

However, any thoughts about God quickly dissipated as we continued with our daily lives. Meanwhile, Mum was still in the process of trying to rebuild her life in Scarborough. When she had received the letter from Dad telling her not to return, it had come as a nasty shock even though it was clear to her that the marriage had not been going well. She found herself stuck in Scarborough at her parents' house, with little more than her clothes, unsure of what to do.

Dad had used the argument that Mum could not have custody of us because she suffered from anxiety and depression and had experienced two breakdowns. The first had been when she was 17, and the second when she was in her late twenties, when I was a toddler, which resulted in one or two short stays on a psychiatric ward.

Needing to rebuild her life, she took a couple of low-paid jobs in Scarborough, the first working for a hat and underwear retailer and the second in a coffee shop. She later left and got a job as a shorthand typist and secretary for Scarborough District Council. She moved into a flat where, on one of our visits to see her, we all shared the same bed, Mum and I sleeping at one end and Andrew at the other.

It is hard for me to imagine just how shattering this experience must have been. She had lost practically everything in one blow. Mum employed a solicitor in an attempt to get custody of us, but Dad was always one step ahead and, having a more capable lawyer, maintained the well-supported argument that Mum wasn't fit to look after us.

During this period she had yet another breakdown, which resulted in being admitted to a psychiatric ward and receiving ECT – electric shock treatment. Initially this appeared to help, in spite of the fact that it impaired her memory for a little while. This was in the days before the wide use of various antipsychotic drugs, and she found some of the sights on the ward disturbing, as the most troubled patients paced up and down, talking to themselves and crying out. Tragically, she was separated from her children, her marriage was over, and she was now confined to a psychiatric ward.

It was not long after the 'raid' that another unannounced change took place in our lives. An agreement had been made that Andrew and I should be allowed to spend some of our school holidays with Mum at Span's house. On one of these occasions, when Dad came to take us home, instead of travelling north to Marton, we were unexpectedly taken south, back to Hornsea, to a new house we hadn't seen before. Dad's new role in the finance company had required him to relocate.

Things must have been looking up for him at this time as the house he had moved into was a new, detached, four-bedroomed property on a modern residential estate. This move meant my brother and I had to change schools. Now we were to attend Hornsea County Primary School, which was partly housed in a large, quite imposing, red-brick building in the town centre. This was my second school and Andrew's third before he had to transfer to secondary school.

On my first day at school, Dad held my hand as we walked along the short pathway leading from the town centre into the school grounds. His hand felt big, warm and comforting, and I felt from this that he cared. I believed at that moment that he loved me. I had a sense that he didn't want me to be unhappy, that he wanted to shelter me from the trauma, but that his choice to live with Ella instead of Mum was something about which he wouldn't or perhaps couldn't compromise. I would never know.

On our trips to see Mum in Scarborough, Dad would drive us to a halfway meeting point in Bridlington where we would be handed over to Mum at the bus station café. We would arrive in Dad's Zephyr, then climb onto a bus with Mum and head for Span and Gramps' house in Scarborough. These trips to Scarborough were our joy, where we bathed in Span's kindness and love and were reunited with Mum.

This light and happiness was always followed by the gloom of our compulsory return to Hornsea. I always had a dread of arriving back at Dad's house. Every mile his car covered took us nearer to a place where we experienced deep unhappiness. Whenever we turned a corner I always hoped it would be in a direction away from the house, to a place which didn't have these negative associations. I wanted the car to keep moving, to never reach its destination but, with mounting dread, I knew it would always take me where I didn't want to go. Every return journey to the house was like this, whether long or short and regardless of where we had been. Although it was a house, it wasn't a home.

Chapter 3
Life with Dad and Ella

It was during this period that I became more aware of Ella's appearance. She couldn't have been more unlike Mum, who was a natural beauty. Ella reminded me of the actress Barbara Windsor, but was less appealing. She was short and buxom, had long, brightly painted fingernails and wore expensive-looking clothes. Around the house she wore high-heeled, fluffy pink slippers. I thought they looked very uncomfortable. She originated from Hartlepool and spoke with an accent similar to a Geordie from Newcastle. She wore thick make-up over her heavy features, but the most startling thing about her looks was that she wore a large, blonde wig in the style of 'big hair', which was fashionable in the 1970s. The bright blonde wig consisted of layered strands of thick, shoulder-length hair which were layered and lightly waved to give a full look. I had no idea at first that it was a wig until one day, when I went upstairs for my weekly bath, I happened to see her without it and noticed that her natural hair consisted of long, wispy, light-coloured strands which grew in thin patches between extensive bald areas. One day, when I had the courage to peek into the master bedroom, I saw a white polystyrene mannequin head perched on Ella's bedside cabinet and surmised it was where she kept her wig after removing it at bedtime.

In our new house my brother and I were given bedrooms on the ground floor while Ella and Dad slept in the master bedroom upstairs. Our bedrooms looked on to the back garden. Owing to the fact that the lawn had been newly seeded, we didn't spend any time playing there, but even after the grass was established we felt we shouldn't go into the back garden. We never spent any time anywhere in the house except for our bedrooms in the evenings and at weekends. We used the downstairs toilet and the kitchen to eat porridge for breakfast and a light meal after school, and once a week I shared a bath with my brother in the upstairs bathroom. The house was nicely decorated and expensively furnished, but we were afraid to go into any of the other rooms, and only ventured into the lounge to say a brief goodnight to Dad before going to bed. This was expected and became our routine.

My relationship with Ella was one of continuous enmity because, having grasped that she had taken over from Mum, I had developed a strong dislike for her. This was mutual and led to much hostility. She had a teenage son who had entered the Forces and occasionally visited our house. He was as unfriendly towards us as his mother was. On one occasion I had angered her so much that she bellowed, 'You needn't bother saying goodnight to ya' father!' I feared Ella so took this to be an order. When the time came to go to bed I didn't take my routine walk through the dining room into the lounge to kiss Dad on the cheek. I thought I was simply doing as I had been told, and that I would get into trouble if I dared to venture into the lounge. But as I lay in bed the bedroom door burst open and Ella dragged me by my hair to say goodnight to Dad in the lounge.

On one occasion Ella accused me of breaking the stem of her rubber plant, which stood in the lounge. I had indeed been in the lounge in the middle of the night to steal a couple of her chocolate mints, but would never have dared so much as to touch the plants, let alone break them. Andrew was also quizzed but neither of us was guilty of this 'crime'. Our denials were not believed so we had to take Ella's punishment, which more often than not was a beating on the legs and bottom. My and my brother's sense of injustice at this false accusation was so profound that it is one of the clearest memories we have of our time with Ella.

On another occasion, there was no toilet paper in the downstairs loo and I had been too afraid to ask Ella for any. As a result, after going to the toilet, I simply pulled my knickers up and carried on my day with a dirty bottom. Even this was preferable to the frightening prospect of approaching Ella. That night I was afraid to tell her that my knickers were dirty so I hid them in my toy cupboard – and there they stayed.

I thought I had managed to avoid getting into trouble, but not long after, Ella made the unpleasant discovery, not just of a soiled pair of knickers in the cupboard, but also of the fact that they were now covered in maggots. She was incensed. My punishment for this was to sit and take my toys out of my cupboard and put them back over and over until she was satisfied I had done it long enough. She didn't bother finding out why I had not asked for toilet paper.

The amount of food Ella gave us was so little when we came home from school that I would often wake up in the night feeling hungry. Since the kitchen was right next to my room I would sneak into it in the small hours of the night, take some slices of bread from the bread bin, smear them with margarine and jam and help myself to various tasty morsels from the biscuit tin. Andrew was, by nature, fairly passive and never joined me in these midnight raids, so I often took what I had stolen to his room and we would share it together. This habit went on for some time until one day Ella discovered crumbs in my bed, for which I received a sound hiding. We weren't properly fed, to the extent that Andrew felt jealous of some local children whose mother gave them milk – something Ella never allowed us to have as a drink at home.

I lived in terror of Ella. She seemed to cut such a frightening figure to me as a young child. After eating our light meal after school of beans or egg on toast, we were expected to help with the washing-up, drying and putting away of plates and cutlery, along with any pans. I was so afraid of Ella I hardly dared open my mouth to speak, even if I needed to. I dreaded having to say 'excuse me' to her when she was standing in front of a cupboard I needed to open to put the plates away. The words stuck in my throat and it often took me an entire washing-up session to build up the courage to ask her to move aside. It was difficult to be in Ella's presence so I came to dread this daily chore.

We were allowed to write to Mum once every few weeks, but our letters were always screened by Ella. We weren't permitted to include anything negative about our lives or what we were experiencing. However, I wanted Mum to know what was happening to us and how unhappy we were. So once I decided to secretly include a note with my letter. Strangely, on this occasion, Ella didn't bother reading our letters, and so they, along with the note, were posted. However, the next day she must have realised her oversight. She summoned me from Andrew's room and asked me about the contents of my letter. To me, Ella appeared to be a towering, all-knowing adult figure and I was sure she must have discovered the secret note, so I instantly confessed. I was afraid of what might happen if I didn't. The resultant punishment for this was severe: a beating and being banned from visiting Mum during the next school holidays.

The threat that we would not be able to visit Mum at Span's house was something that always hung over us. Ella knew this was the most effective way to keep us toeing the line because we lived in eager anticipation of our holidays there. Whether Ella knew it or not, this was the surest way to compound our misery and add to the distress of our situation.

On another occasion I had arrived at my grandmother's house for the holidays when Mum discovered that my bottom was black and blue, covered in bruises from a hiding I had received from Ella. She wanted to show it to the neighbour who was a nurse, but I felt too embarrassed to show my bare bottom to someone I didn't know, so the incident passed without any further action or comment.

My brother also received beatings, though not as often. His nature was different to mine and he was keen to avoid trouble. I was the one viewed as difficult, so more often bore the brunt of Ella's anger. However, Andrew once refused to take Blackie, Dad and Ella's dog, for a walk, so Ella launched herself at him as he sat on his bed, grabbing him by the throat and digging her long nails into his neck, causing him to scream. Dad and I were also in the room, standing nearby. I looked on, frightened. Dad's response was to gently escort me into my own bedroom so I wouldn't have to witness any more. I was sure I too would be punished and that Dad would allow Ella to deal with us in whatever way she judged best. He then removed himself from the scene. Throughout our ordeal Dad stood by, passive and uninvolved. He himself never once hit us, but he did not intervene to stop Ella from doing so.

Quite what Dad was experiencing during these years wasn't clear to me. Although we were living in the same house, we were practically strangers – our only memorable and regular contact being the goodnight kiss in the lounge. Yet occasionally I would hear him at night, sobbing loudly upstairs. To my young ears it was a strange sound – hearing a grown man cry. It seemed to come from deep within him – like an agonising pain. I felt afraid as I lay in my bed listening to it and was surprised by the fact that he didn't seem to care whether I heard or not. The emotional distance between us was too great for me to even contemplate running upstairs to him. I lay in the dark, alone with the sense that I could never cross the chasm between me and Dad. My life was being lived in almost total isolation from his, and I was helpless to make anything better.

How this situation affected me and my brother is hard to assess, but certainly the medication incident showed we were deeply unhappy. Interestingly, it is now known that a child's manner of play reveals their inner world and how they are feeling. No one did, but had anyone watched me alone at play, they might have had cause for concern.

I owned a couple of large baby dolls and two smaller dolls, one of which came complete with a set of three wigs – Ella's way of diverting me away from my fascination with hers. Most girls would have enjoyed these toys, but I hated my dolls. I would pick them up by one leg and throw them viciously around my bedroom, draw cuts on their arms and legs with a red felt-tip pen and, using string, hang them by the neck from my door handle. I wanted to inflict as much pain and misery on my dolls as I could. I felt good when I beat them, as if they were now getting some of what I had received from Ella.

With my teddy bears, however, it was quite the opposite. I made cosy beds for them, tucking them up at night. I loved them. They represented animals, unlike the dolls which were modelled on people, and it was people – Ella in particular – who were inflicting the pain I was experiencing. I could trust animals. They were always the same and never vindictive. They wouldn't hurt me, whereas people would.

The fact the dolls were female somehow tied in with Ella's hatred of me. Being a girl myself, this translated into a form of self-loathing and into a dislike of girlishness. As a result of this and, not having a positive female role model to look up to, I became quite tomboyish and competitive, always wanting to be the fastest, toughest girl. I rarely wore dresses and have no memory of having my hair fussed over. I joined my brother when he played with his electric train set and, like him, began to collect matchbox cars. I often sat in bed making 'hills' with my knees while steering the cars around make-believe, exotic 'countries'. This was one of my favourite forms of play. I despised girly girls or girls who liked playing with dolls or who were scared to do daring things. I considered them to be weak and silly.

Yet, secretly, most nights I cried myself to sleep while lying on my stomach in bed. All I wanted was Mum and Dad to be together again with us, under the same roof. I clung to this dream, sure that it would happen. The possibility that it might not was inconceivable at the time.

No one ever came to check on me at night and I was left to process these thoughts and feelings on my own. The only person who could understand was Andrew, but he was on the other side of my bedroom wall. Although we were all living in the same house there seemed to be invisible yet thick walls, even chasms, between us which could never be crossed. No one spoke about feelings or counselled us in any way. Life seemed to be simply about going from one day to the next in a matter-of-fact way, doing what needed to be done, but with no heartfelt connections, no hugs, never an 'I love you'. The only close relationship I had was with Andrew. We had a toy telephone set which Mum had bought us and we were allowed to rig it up between our bedrooms. We often used these phones to talk to each other from our rooms. This was a lifeline, a way of alleviating our distress and isolation.

Deep down I knew my brother and I were being neglected. I knew we weren't being cared for the way children should be. One day I was visiting Dad's adoptive mum, who had become known to us as Grandma Webster. She lived in an old, dark, terraced house, just minutes from the seafront in Hornsea. I was eight years old and was walking alone to visit her when I noticed a baby in a pram. The pram was in the front garden of another terraced house a few doors down from Grandma Webster's. The front garden was tiny, as were all the front gardens on this road – it couldn't have been more than four square metres – just a small concrete area fronted by a low wall and a wooden gate.

The baby was sitting in a large, raised-up pram of the kind commonly used in those days. It looked so happy, so clean and well-fed, so cared for. Deep down I knew I wasn't cared for like that and suddenly felt a surge of jealousy and resentment. I stopped and glanced up and down the quiet street. There was no one looking, so I quickly pushed open the gate, stepped onto the concrete garden area, raised my right hand and aimed the hardest slap I could muster against the baby's soft, chubby left cheek. I then watched with relish as the baby reacted, first with an expression of shock, and then, a few seconds later, with a loud cry, at which point I turned and sprinted a few metres to an alleyway. The alley led to a rough track which ran between the backs of the houses, enabling me to enter Grandma's back garden unobserved.

I knew what I had done was wrong, but it seemed to satisfy something in me – that justice had somehow been served. Now I wasn't the only one who was hurt and unhappy. I enjoyed the fact that someone else who had done nothing to deserve it had been on the receiving end of another person's vindictiveness. I wanted the baby to learn that life can be cruel, that people cause pain and that not everyone would love it, just as I had discovered at a young age that not everyone loved me.

One day, Ella gave me a hiding for something I had done. I sat on my bed, glaring up at her and scowling as she stood in front of me. Then it happened – a pivotal moment in my life had arrived; one which would shape my personality. The beating had made me want to cry. I was shaking with the strain of holding back the tears, but I knew I must never let *her* see that. There and then I resolved I would never let her see me cry. I would never let *anyone* see me cry. I would never be weak or a victim, I would fight. I would always be strong. I knew from now on I had to help myself if I was going to survive. As I sat continuing to scowl at Ella, I promised myself that no one would ever turn me into a victim, no one would ever defeat me, I would survive no matter what. My self-image became shaped by this defining moment. I began to build a hard wall around myself, one which no one would ever get through to hurt me again. I would be independent. I would do what needed to be done. *I* would do it, without having to rely on anyone. After all, how could I rely on other people when I felt I had been badly let down by them?

Yet there was some kindness in our lives outside of Mum and Span. Our visits to Grandma Webster were always ones where we experienced care, albeit in an austere form. Grandma Webster didn't exhibit quite the same warmth as Span, but she was never unkind. Our regular visits would take place in her dark back room, a sitting room-cum-dining area which was situated between the front lounge and the kitchen at the back. The furniture in the room was made from dark wood, and a coal fire usually burned in the hearth. A little light came in from the window, which looked out on to the narrow back garden and the side of the kitchen. As well as the smell from the coal fire, there was generally a strong, fusty aroma which I later came to learn was the scent of mothballs clinging to Grandma Webster's clothes.

She always wore woolly, straight skirts and clumpy, black shoes, which looked a bit like clogs but had laces which crisscrossed the length of the shoes, giving them a boot-like appearance. Under these she wore thick, light-brown tights which gathered in wrinkles around the front of her ankles. During our visits we used to play dominoes on a green felt table, and would visit the outside toilet when the need arose.

Grandma Webster always prepared a light tea for us, and invariably part of this would be the strange combination of brown bread and butter served alongside tinned mandarin oranges. I could never understand why she was so fond of this culinary mix, as bread and mandarins didn't seem to go at all well together, but we never protested and always ate whatever she put in front of us. Then every time, as we were leaving, she gave Andrew and me a big Victoria penny each, pressing the coins into our hands and then folding our fingers tightly over them as if to say, 'These are yours and no one else's.'

As a birthday gift she gave me two books about Bible characters: *The Story of Joseph* and *The Story of David* by Mary Alice Jones. I felt these stories were somehow different to my other books because they were taken from the Bible, but my understanding was very hazy and it didn't occur to me that they could have relevance for my life.

It seemed as though our lives would continue on like this indefinitely. Neither Dad nor Ella nor Grandma Webster had ever sat down with us to explain why our lives were this way, nor what the future expectations might be. As a result we could not have known that our days visiting Grandma Webster were numbered; that soon we would be parted from her forever.

Chapter 4
A dream come true

The decision had been made that we would now be allowed to live with Mum. Although I only came to learn of it many years later, Dad had written to her saying that Ella could not go on any longer under the circumstances and was threatening to leave. He went on to say that my brother and I would be placed in a children's home if Mum were unable or unwilling to take us.

From this, it appeared that Dad had chosen Ella over me and Andrew, which might well have been the case. However, in fairness, these were times when flexible working hours and paternity leave were virtually unheard of. It would have been impossible for Dad to look after us on his own while holding down a responsible full-time job. Added to that was the fact that in the 1960s and 1970s, raising and caring for children was still seen as primarily women's work. Perhaps it was the realisation that he was heading for this inevitable outcome that had caused his loud, nocturnal sobbing. I would never know.

Realising that we were to leave Dad's house and live with Mum, my happiness knew no bounds. As Andrew and I packed up our clothes and toys in dazed disbelief at a dream come true, it was as if a dark veil were being lifted from my life. No one came to my room as I packed my things, so I was left alone with my excited anticipation at the thought of a new and happier life.

Once installed in Span's little bungalow I felt as though my inner being were bathing in glorious sunlight. So unexpectedly, warmth, joy and love had flooded into my life. It didn't matter that we were now living in a tiny property, crammed four to a bedroom on camp beds, or that we didn't have a car. I was with the people who loved me. I no longer had to live in fear of Ella. I was free. Such was my happiness and excitement that I did not give much thought to how Dad might be feeling. At ten years of age I was too young to do so.

Span and Gramps' bungalow was situated on a windswept, elevated stretch of coastline south of Scarborough and a 20-minute walk from cliffs which, covered in flora, sloped down to the beach. The elevation meant that the bungalow was buffeted by strong winds blowing off the cold North Sea, especially in winter. On this stretch of coastline grey, cloudy weather was the norm, but occasionally there would be a beautiful, clear, sunny day with gentle winds, which would cause Span's bungalow to take on an exciting holiday feel.

Though small, her home was always clean and tidy, her sheets and towels aromatically fresh, having been blown dry by the maritime winds. In the lounge, which doubled as a dining area, she had a small, dark wood, foldaway table. When there were extra people to feed, it would be pulled out and unfolded and chairs would be fetched from the kitchen and bedrooms. Span cooked well – plain but tasty and wholesome meals. At teatime she invariably produced a fresh salad to be eaten with ham, cheese and boiled eggs, followed by teacakes, bread, jam and fruit cake. The fresh smell of cucumber reliably informed me that food was served. Meals around Span's table, though crowded, were happy times of family and belonging. The days of being confined to our bedrooms and eating alone in the kitchen were now just a bad and rapidly fading memory.

Span, a former nurse, was an attractive-looking woman – fair-skinned, fine-featured and quietly spoken. She was of average height with broad shoulders and was generally strong, but sadly she suffered from varicose veins and bunions. Her eyes usually looked pink-rimmed and watery, caused by the cold wind on her eyelids. Her hands were red and chapped from domestic work, much of which was washing laundry by hand, after which she would squeeze the wet garments flat through a wooden mangle, the water pouring into a waiting bucket. She always wore tights and had a habit of stroking her knees. Whenever her hands came into contact with her tights there would be a crackling sound as the dry skin caught on the nylon threads. She would often read to me as I sat on her knee, and I would look at her red hands and how they creased around the thumb joint while she held the book where we both could see it.

Span, in contrast to Gramps, who was quite mean-spirited and domineering, was sweet-natured and generous to a fault. 'You should always treat animals kindly,' she would instruct me while stroking her Labrador-cross, Candy, or placing a saucer of milk outside for the neighbour's cat.

The nearby cliffs and beach became familiar places to me. Accompanied by Mum, Span and Andrew I would follow a mud track which began at the coast road and led down towards the cliffs. The path then split into two, the left side following the clifftop several miles all the way into Scarborough and the track on the right leading down through a wooded area onto the beaches which stretched to Cayton Bay and beyond. Here, Andrew and I would climb a high cliff, named by locals as Camel's Hump, which jutted out towards the sea. From the top it provided a sweeping panorama of the coastline as far as Scarborough and its medieval castle, the latter giving the town its distinctive skyline. Along the beach we explored the Second World War air-raid shelters, hollow blocks of concrete with narrow, horizontal 'windows' which served as places from which to observe and shoot the enemy. In Scarborough itself we would often be taken to the outdoor swimming pools, spending the whole day there, accompanied by Span or Mum, and then return home to a delicious teatime meal.

Compared to my experiences living with Ella and Dad, these were golden days full of enjoyment. But we knew they couldn't go on forever. The bungalow was simply too small to house five people for an indefinite period. At the same time, Dad had decided to sue for divorce and Mum had no money to buy a property of her own. The houses we had lived in while with Dad had all been in his name and since, at the time, there didn't appear to be legislation which entitled Mum to a share of the possessions, Dad kept everything, including the furniture.

A court order was eventually put in place which stated Dad had to pay a monthly amount towards our upkeep. He paid £3.50 per week towards Mum's upkeep and £1.20 per week towards ours. It wasn't a great deal of money even in the 1970s.

I was temporarily placed at Wheatcroft Primary School, a few miles from Span's house on the road to Scarborough town centre and just minutes from Scarborough's picturesque South Cliff area. But I was only there for six weeks before being moved to Cayton County Primary School, which was closer. It was situated in a pretty village a few miles outside of Scarborough, and a ten-minute cycle ride from Span's house. I joined the school in what today would be Year 5. It was my fourth primary school, and by now I was used to being 'the new girl', having to join in with children who had settled into the school years before I arrived. Of necessity, I learned to swiftly make friends and find my way around new environments.

Mum bought me a red bicycle since now, aged ten, I was allowed to cycle to school alone. I loved the long, steep, exhilarating downhill run along the winding country road which led into Cayton village.

School was a happy place for me. Here there was order, normality and clear boundaries. Things were done systematically. At school assembly it was the norm to sing Christian songs such as 'Jesus wants me for a sunbeam'. I liked the words, which evoked a cheerful image of yellow rays, but didn't understand what it meant to be a sunbeam for Jesus. Before lunch we would pray corporately, 'For what we are about to receive, may the Lord make us truly thankful.' Again, these words were pleasant and comforting, yet I felt that any God who existed must be impersonal and far off.

I felt safe at school, and my confidence began to grow as, eager to please, I set about my studies and played lots of sport. I joined the school rounders team, becoming known as one of the 'sloggers' as my right arm sent the ball sailing over the heads of the opposition. In this way I began to experience approval and a sense of achievement. I particularly enjoyed art and writing, throwing myself into long projects on the Romans, and on hamsters.

Yet I felt embarrassed and ashamed that my dad was not living with us. All the friends I made at school came from Cayton and surrounding villages where both parents were still together. Not wanting to stand out as different from my peers, I lied about Dad's whereabouts, saying he worked away from home. This deception would be hard to maintain over the long term, but it served the initial purpose of saving face.

Although my life now was so much better, I carried around a vague feeling of being cast adrift. I was acutely aware of the lack of an ongoing father figure in my life. Although Gramps was around, he wasn't an especially hands-on grandfather and was easily irritated. As we no longer lived with Dad I wouldn't see him or hear him coming into the house or even have an awareness of his presence, albeit from a distance. It was as though the last vestiges of an anchor had been pulled up and removed. I felt I now had no right to look to him for anything.

In addition, I was aware of a shadow: Dad's disapproval, caused by the belief I had let him down, that I had shattered his plans for us to live with him and Ella.

This made me feel like a bad person of little worth, that I didn't deserve to be loved, that I wasn't as good as the other children because their parents were still living together and mine weren't.

Seeing myself in this way I was surprised that my form teacher, Mr Land, appeared to approve of me. He often affirmed me with positive feedback on my school work and, as a result, I latched on to him, eagerly drawing off his encouragement and acceptance of me. So, probably unknown to him, he became a significant person in my life. When he selected me to represent the school in art and to recite a Pam Ayres poem about hedgehogs at a school concert, I endeavoured to do my very best. I wanted to please Mr Land – his approval was very important to me – and it helped to make up for the fact I didn't have Dad's backing.

When it came to the school concert in which I was to recite the poem, I scanned the audience: a sea of parents' faces. Crestfallen, I saw that neither Mum nor Span were there. I couldn't believe it. I had worked so hard on my poem. Where *were* they? Wasn't my performance worth watching? Wasn't *I* worth watching? Suddenly, I didn't want to recite the poem. What was the point if the people who really mattered weren't there?

But as I stood up and walked centre stage to do my recitation, my eyes fell on Mr Land, who was standing in my line of view at the back of the hall, arms folded, looking happy and relaxed, his iron-grey hair in its usual style, oiled and slicked back off his florid face. He was wearing a broad, very satisfied grin as I went through the routine he had invested so much time in teaching me. I realised that there *was* someone I could perform for, someone who *was* interested in what I was about to do. It wasn't quite like being watched by Mum or Span, but it was enough to make a difference. I sensed that he was proud of me.

And yet, in spite of these positives, the impact of my childhood trauma was all too evident. The independence that had been so vital to my survival was now a marked feature of my character and would play a significant influence in the trajectory of my life, not least in my friendships.

My closest friends at the school were Jill and Shirley. Thanks to Mum, who paid for me to have occasional riding lessons, I had developed a keen interest in horses. Consequently I loved going to Jill's house because her family owned a number of ponies which grazed on a one-acre plot behind their bungalow.

I liked to think Jill, Shirley and I were equally close as a threesome, but inside I had my doubts. The wall I had built when I was younger was still intact. Did it make me hard to get to know? Did I hold back my true thoughts and feelings from people so that no one could hurt me, and to be certain that I wouldn't appear weak and vulnerable? Did I come across as *so* independent I didn't really need anyone?

My place in the friendship pecking order was confirmed at Jill's birthday party. We had been asked to come in fancy dress and I had set about a fairly ambitious plan to make a ghost outfit. This consisted of a white, brushed cotton sheet which I had spent hours and hours cutting, stitching and stuffing. It was a labour of love, and I had poured myself into it.

At the party I arrived, proud to be wearing my creation. I knew the only other serious contender would be Shirley because, like me, she was closer to Jill than the other children were. She had dressed herself up as a punk rocker, achieving the look with a loud assortment of clothes, jewellery and make-up. The effect was impressive, but I knew it could never have taken up anything like the time and effort I had poured into my ghost. Surely the judge, Jill's mum, would realise that.

But no. Shirley was chosen. I felt so cheated and wanted to cry at what I saw as the injustice of it, as Jill's mum walked over to me and jokingly pushed my consolation prize, a small chocolate bar, through one of my costume's eye holes. It was such a relief that my face was covered as I stuffed down the tears which were ready to burst forth. I was devastated, perhaps more so because I felt this told me that first prize had very little to do with the costumes and far more to do with the fact that Jill was a closer friend to Shirley than she was to me.

Often I questioned whether any of the many friends I had made at various schools were real friends after all. How well did all these people actually know me? Walking across the school field during playtime one day I passed a group of four girls walking along, arms linked, loudly singing a song from the popular music charts. I looked contemptuously at them, sure that this vocal strutting was designed to impress. But then a disturbing thought entered my mind. I knew I wouldn't link arms like that with any of *my* friends. I wouldn't feel comfortable allowing them to get that close. It would, in fact, be embarrassing.

My independence meant I was happy in my own company, sometimes going off alone to the nearby cliffs. I loved the open space and the untamed power of the sea. The roar of its waters and the seagulls' cries became etched in my psyche as sounds associated with my childhood. I found solace in nature. Although the sea was vast and continuously moving, it remained the same – always changing but never changed. Amid all the vicissitudes of my young life, here was something that appeared consistent.

Before long, though, our current accommodation arrangements had to change, as we had known they would. For practical reasons – not to mention Gramps' impatience and annoyance at having young children living under his roof – we would need to find a home of our own. As a result, another change would soon be coming, one which marked the onset of a phase as challenging as the one my brother and I had been through with Dad and Ella.

Chapter 5
Our new home

While I was still at primary school in Cayton, Mum was offered a local authority house, situated about one mile inland from Span's bungalow. It was at Eastfield, one of the largest council estates in North Yorkshire, built in a semi-rural district several miles south of Scarborough.

The design of the house was typical of council housing across the country. It had three bedrooms, a lounge, or 'front room' as we called it, and a kitchen-diner at the back. Through the back door of the kitchen-diner was a coal house which we named the 'back spot'. A space for storing coal was situated at the far end, but we only used the back spot as a place to keep a few gardening tools and our bikes.

The front garden was little more than a small rectangle of overgrown grass, surrounded by a large privet hedge, with a small gate; the back garden was again small and uncultivated. A large, grey, tin coal bunker stood just in front of the kitchen window. We stored our coal here, sliding up a ground-level metal plate at the front to access it and filling a pink coal scuttle which we then carried through the house into the front room where we used the coal to make a fire. Our dustbin was a metal one, large and round, with a matching lid. I recall the harsh metallic scraping sound it made as, once a week, we would drag it through the passage which ran between our house and the neighbour's. It was then the job of the dustmen to heave the heavy bins onto their backs and deposit the mix of foul-smelling rubbish into the back of a truck.

Upstairs there were three bedrooms and, once again, I was given the box room which overlooked the road. My toys, including the big, golden-yellow teddy bear, were all piled onto a large, square box-shelf which took up about a quarter of the space in the room. Andrew's larger room was next to mine, and Mum had the back bedroom, a dark room which received little sun. A small bathroom and separate toilet were situated at the top of the stairs.

Social services provided all the furniture and furnishings, which came to us second-hand – even the carpets. I looked at the motley mismatch of colours we had been allocated: a grey carpet with multicoloured markings on it, a fawn-coloured sofa with black piping round the edges, two matching armchairs and an old piano with ugly brass candlesticks attached to either side of its front panel. Eventually, a black and white television came to stand in the corner.

There was no telephone, central heating or double-glazing – just a single pane of glass between us and the North Sea winds which battered the coastline. On very cold winter mornings a thin layer of ice would form on the inside of the glass. There was a vent in the top left-hand corner of the front wall in my bedroom. This area regularly became dark with mildew as damp seeped through the wall, and no matter how many times we papered over it, the black stain always recurred, causing the wallpaper to peel away. Occasionally woodlice would crawl through the vent. I would try to stop this, but they kept coming, and sometimes I had the unpleasant experience of waking in the morning to find one of them making its way across my pillow.

Keeping warm in the house during winter was a challenge. My bedding consisted of two flat sheets, three or four blankets and a thin bedspread which, when I awoke in the mornings, had often tumbled to the floor. I had a small, portable two-bar electric fire in my room, but this could not be left on all night, so when I awoke in the mornings the air in the room was sometimes so cold I could see my own breath.

On dark winter mornings when I got up for school, I would pick up my uniform, pull on my dressing gown and head downstairs to the kitchen. Lighting the little gas fire and holding one by one the cold pieces of my school uniform in front of it, I would then quickly slip each garment on, momentarily enjoying the delicious sensation of warmth against my skin.

Bathing would take place once a week on a Sunday night. To obtain hot water we had to light the gas boiler in the kitchen and wait between 30 minutes and one hour for the water in the loft tank to heat up sufficiently to half-fill the bath.

At first we heated the front room by making a coal fire. For this we needed to make paper kindling by rolling, then twisting, sheets of newspaper which we placed under and around pieces of coal. Keeping the fireplace clean and tidy, however, was an onerous task, and eventually the open fire was boarded up and fronted by a modern gas appliance.

To our great delight and excitement, our black and white TV was later replaced by a colour one.

Although I was always happy to be away from Ella, our struggles were far from over. Other than the money Dad was ordered to pay every month, we lived on benefits doled out by the State. These were sufficient for the basics of life, but little more. We became accustomed to the fact that life was a struggle. Mum would often complain about how hard everything was, and how doing anything seemed to require so much effort as we didn't have the means, such as a car or sufficient disposable income. As children, Andrew and I were more accepting of the situation and got used to walking, catching buses and cycling. I have vivid memories of looking at my hands turning a bluish-purple colour as I rode my bike up and down hills against the freezing wind and rain.

During the years we lived at Eastfield, Dad visited us once every six months: in July for my brother's birthday and in December for mine. Now that we were living apart, which I really believed was my doing, I usually felt quite anxious about his visits. Although I wanted to see him, when he actually appeared I often felt tongue-tied, not only unsure of what to say but having trouble saying it. Over the years his input into my life had been so minimal that I struggled to find common ground with him.

His visits developed a routine: prior to his arrival we cleaned and tidied the house, bought more food than usual and put on our smartest clothes. Dad, always well-dressed, would arrive in a company car and, after being let in, would sit in the kitchen and drink tea, while we sat looking at him, unsure of what to say. He would give us £5 each, then Andrew and I would get into his car to be driven into town. Dad wasn't the type to enjoy outdoor activities so his outings with us were always into Scarborough town centre to watch over us as we spent our £5.

On one of these occasions he asked me, 'What would you like to buy, a dress or something?'

'A dress?' I snorted. I found the notion of a dress alien, even embarrassing. I didn't wear dresses. I was far too tomboyish for that. If Dad was hoping to cultivate my femininity, he had left it rather late. I could see he appeared taken aback by my curt response. Unhappy about my reaction, I tried to soften it by suggesting an alternative.

On his visits, such conversation as there was concentrated on external matters, and nothing pertaining to the heart. Once or twice he informed me that he thought I was hard, adding that I was even harder than him. I hated being told this because it reinforced my belief that I was bad.

Over and beyond that and the fact I had seemingly put a stop to his plans for Andrew and me to live with him and Ella, I didn't really know what he thought of me. Dad never spoke affectionately to me. Feelings and heartfelt longings were never discussed. Indeed, it would have felt counter-intuitive, even dangerous, to go there. Throughout our childhood Andrew and I had never been encouraged to verbally express our emotions. Strong feelings were simmering just below the surface, but it seemed safer not to pay heed to them. Who knew what might have happened if we had dared to venture there and someone had said the wrong thing?

As a result I had little, if any, idea about what Dad was thinking or feeling. I found myself having to constantly second-guess him and read between the lines. I couldn't understand, for example, why on one occasion he threw his bi-annual gift of £5 at me, as if angered by the fact that he was expected to give me something. Did he perhaps think I only wanted his money? Did he resent giving me anything at all? I felt shocked and hurt but had no idea what to say or do next, so I simply sat and looked at him. Then it came out: 'I've had to earn every penny I own and *you* can do the same,' he snapped at me. All I could glean from this was that he never intended to give me anything over and above the regular £5 and that I shouldn't expect anything more from him. So I didn't.

Dad put on a good show of holding everything together when he was visiting us, but on one occasion as he was leaving, he reached the garden gate and suddenly let out a loud, uncontrolled sob – the same sound I had heard coming from his bedroom as I lay in my bed in Hornsea. I stood in the house doorway, staring at his back, rooted to the spot, as he opened the rickety garden gate. I was surprised, as I had always been, to suddenly hear him cry – and within my earshot. It didn't fit with his steely, businesslike approach towards us when he came to visit. I stood, frozen, not knowing how to react. I could tell from his posture, from the fact that he just kept walking, that he didn't expect any response from me.

We were growing increasingly further apart, not only because we no longer lived under the same roof but also because there was no sharing of hearts and minds. It was as if the barrier which had stood between us at his house was now wider than ever, preventing me from giving Dad a hug and vice versa. I had no idea how to remove it. I could only watch as he disappeared behind the garden hedge, and I felt helpless to do anything except to simply close the door.

Chapter 6
Single-parent family

As Dad had never been very hands-on, I didn't miss him much. Nevertheless, there was always a sense of incompleteness, that something, or rather someone, vital was missing. My dream that my parents would live together again, that we would be a 'normal' family, had by now died.

The presence and meaningful provision of a father was no longer there. Mum had to carry the full load for raising us and was all too aware of our lack. She acquired a puppy from some local people so that we would feel more like a family. As a result, a chocolate brown collie-cross, Mick, became an important and integral part of our home life. He was later joined by a series of hamsters and Dickie the budgerigar.

As the months went by, Mum simply kept going, putting one foot in front of the other. She did not have a job outside the home and her days were spent keeping house and walking to the local parade of shops to buy our daily food requirements. I regularly saw her trudging back along the path, carrying two heavy plastic bags filled with groceries. It never occurred to me to offer to help; I was too selfish for that. As soon as she came home I would pounce on the bags, pull out any tasty treats and disappear into the front room to eat them on my own.

She continued to suffer from anxiety and nerves and had a facial twitch. Her upper lip would contort uncontrollably and draw stares from people when we were on the bus or in other public places. I found this embarrassing, but was protective of Mum and wanted to defend her, so I would fix with an angry glare anyone who stared at her for too long. 'Who are they to judge?' I would angrily reason to myself, and felt sorely tempted to verbally abuse them. Deep down I was seething, but never stopped to ask myself why.

Sometimes at night I would hear Mum sobbing in her bedroom, in much the same way I had heard Dad cry. I knew that, on and off, she was taking an antidepressant. After meals I would sometimes see her place a prescription tablet in her mouth, take a mouthful of water and throw her head back to swallow it. I had heard the word 'depression' but wasn't clear about what it was. 'It's this house,' Mum often complained, 'it makes me feel depressed.' I wanted to do something about her crying. I wanted to put a stop to her unhappiness, but I felt immobilised, incapable of dealing with it; I was almost embarrassed at the thought I might have to express some care and affection for her. These things had never been modelled to me so I simply responded in the way I had been shown – by saying nothing or being very matter of fact.

Occasionally she would smoke a cigarette to calm her nerves. I was afraid of what the cigarettes might do to her health. I wanted her to stop and would hunt around the house until I found where she had hidden the packet of ten, then would destroy the cigarettes and throw them in the bin. It was strange for someone my age to be exercising guardianship over my own mother, but I wanted her to recover fully and be happy. More to the point, who else would help her? Yet, as with so many difficult things in our lives, I felt my childish efforts were largely ineffectual and didn't know how to improve things.

Every few months a social worker came to our home to ask questions about how our lives were going. In time we came to regard these visits as a complete waste of time. We were aware that we faced many financial, practical and emotional problems, but the visits from the social worker made no difference to these. Nothing ever changed for the better following her visits; no plan of action was ever put in place, and we simply struggled on.

Aged ten, I was a slim, taller than average girl. Although born black-haired, my hair colour had changed and now I had long, dark blonde locks which usually hung in long rats' tails down my back. I wasn't very conscious of my appearance and spent very little time tidying my hair. It clearly looked unsightly, as I remember Gramps on one occasion pulling out a comb when he met me in the street and trying to sort through the tangles.

I was described as quiet, shy and sensible by teachers. Yet unknown to them there was a latent anger in me which could erupt under provocation. Not having the backing of a father, I felt I had to fight my own battles. So whenever a threatening situation arose I believed I only had myself to depend on. My past had taught me that if something was wrong, I alone had to be the one to put it right.

One day, in my last year of primary school, I was sitting on a high wall at the school bus stop when one of my friends walked past. A few hours earlier we had had a minor falling-out. Now words were exchanged and an argument erupted. After a brief altercation she turned to continue on her way but, unexpectedly, I suddenly felt very angry. I wouldn't allow her to speak to me like that! I leaped off the wall, ran to her and swung my right arm with as much force as I could, bringing the underside of my fist hard across her left ear. Since she didn't strike back but simply turned and walked away, that put an end to the conflict, and I felt satisfied that I had gained justice for myself.

On another occasion, when Andrew was in his early teens and I was 11, he had invited a friend to our house. The friend was about 14 and lived across the road from us. He was upstairs on the landing outside my room, crouching on the floor during some sort of activity with my brother, when he said something which I felt was meant to provoke me.

I looked down at him, sizing him up. He had very prominent cheekbones, deep-set brown eyes and dark, tousled hair which fell over his forehead. He stared intently up at me as if challenging me to retaliate. Would I back down or would I rise to his provocation? I retorted verbally and, not wanting to now lose face – and against my better judgement, as he was bigger than me – I thumped him hard with my right fist across his left cheekbone. Knowing there would be a bad reaction, I instantly turned and fled down the stairs, trying to prevent myself from falling by running my left hand along the wall.

He was too quick, though. Hot on my heels, he hurled his full weight against my back, causing the inside of my wrist to scrape against the wall, sending shooting pains up my arm. It was excruciating but I believed it had been worth it. I had stood up for myself and, in spite of my injury, I felt I had won.

As children in a single-parent family, Andrew and I had to grow up and become independent more quickly than would otherwise have been the case. There was no sense of being carried along or cosseted in any way. We had to make our own entertainment, which essentially for me was outdoor activities such as cycling, swimming, walking Mick, riding horses and spending time with school friends. I also liked to watch television and do a bit of gardening, which included creating a small flowerbed and vegetable patch where I sometimes grew potatoes and carrots. Andrew rode his bike and set about making a go-kart, complete with car battery and headlamp. Other than that, he spent time in his room or wandered around the estate with friends.

As Mum was busy at home much of the time I had a lot more freedom than most girls my age. Bordering on being a feral child, I more or less came and went as I pleased. This liberty, however, had the potential to lead me into some risky situations.

I would walk in lonely places with Mick, such as an isolated mile-long track which led upwards from the steep dip near our house, known as 'the dell', to a war monument called Oliver's Mount, which overlooked Scarborough.

One day I was sitting on a grassy rise near the track, my arm round Mick, enjoying the view, when I heard a snapping sound behind me. I turned to look and saw a man watching me. He was standing about eight metres away in a ploughed field on the other side of a wire perimeter fence. He smiled at me then turned to carry on his way. I wondered what he was doing walking along the edge of a ploughed field when there was a perfectly good track nearby. I speculated he had come from a nearby home for mentally disturbed people. This thought put me on my guard. Thinking he had gone, I continued to sit for a few more minutes, somewhat apprehensively now, when I heard another snapping noise. I turned again and there he was again, standing in the same spot, staring at me.

I needed no more warning. Stories I had heard as a young child about the 'bogeyman' and a scary film we had watched at school about dangerous strangers now came into play. I knew this was a risky situation and, without wasting another second, sped off down the grassy rise in the direction of the track, Mick running alongside, barking excitedly. I ran as fast as I could, my feet drumming against the hard, dry mud. It felt like a bad dream in which I was running hard but not reaching my destination fast enough. I was sure the stranger must be hot on my heels and, too frightened to look back, I tore to the end of the track, up the broad, gravel pathway to the top of the dell and finally to the road and safety. I didn't stop running until I shot through our front door. Finding Andrew in the hallway I told him what had happened, but he appeared unconcerned. He didn't want to listen, so I had to process this disturbing episode on my own.

At the age of 11, I occasionally cycled to Filey, the neighbouring town, a seven-mile ride along the coast. I saw it as a big adventure to cycle there and back on my own. These were the days when farmers burned stubble in their fields, and it was on a cycle ride to Filey that I encountered one of these fires. The wind was blowing the thick, black stubble-smoke across the road. It was directly in my path but I assumed I was looking at a narrow band of smoke I could quickly ride through. Holding my breath, I ploughed on, entering the smoke. It was dark grey and intermingled with charred wisps of stubble. I screwed up my eyes against the stinging heat of the smoke, thinking that at any minute I would emerge into the fresh air – but this didn't happen. There appeared to be no end to the smoke, and I began to fear not being able to breathe. Turning round seemed to present as much of a problem as going on because I had already travelled some distance. I felt I had no choice but to carry on, not knowing when the smoke would end.

This scary episode ended when suddenly the smoke cleared and I found myself back in the fresh air. Besmirched by the soot and shaken up by the thought of what might have happened if the smoke had gone on much longer, I continued on my way, having learned never to cycle through smoke again.

Not having a resident father meant I frequently had to compensate for this lack by doing things a girl my age would not normally do. For example, one evening a school friend, who was also from a single-parent family, had been at our house. When it was time for her to go home, she said she was afraid to walk alone in the dark through the dell.

This was an isolated area away from the houses, so I offered to walk her through it. I would then have to walk the same route alone to get home. The irony of this was not lost on me, but my self-image was such that I brushed aside any doubts about this arrangement – after all, I was the tough, independent one, and other girls were weaklings – or so I had come to believe since my days with Ella. This was how I had come to see myself, and I intended to live up to it.

Although I was very happy to be living with Mum and away from Ella, I didn't like living on the council estate. Having lived with Dad and then at Span's house, I had something to compare it with. I understood this wasn't a desirable place to be, that there was a stigma attached to such places, that people on council estates were viewed as being second class.

I often walked or cycled the one mile to Span's house, and the route took me through a private housing area which backed on to the council estate. The private estate began a couple of hundred metres along the road from our house. Cycling or walking along, I would cross this invisible line where the council houses ended and the private ones began, and I would notice a change in atmosphere which was almost tangible.

On reflection, the private houses were actually fairly small and ordinary, but when I compared them with where I was living, they appeared almost palatial. Unlike the dull brown bricks of the council houses, the bricks of these houses were of cheerful, lighter colours. The council houses were identical in design, but the private ones varied in size and shape. The gardens on the council estate were often unkempt or littered with old cars, sofas, mattresses and general junk. Gates and fences, including our own, were dilapidated. The front gardens of the private houses were neat and planted out with flowers and shrubs. The roads and paths on the council estate were often littered with broken glass or soiled by dog excrement, but in the private area everything appeared to be neat, clean and fresh. Stray dogs often roamed the streets on the council estate, including our own dog, Mick, who sometimes slipped through our hands and shot down the passage from the back garden to take himself off for a run. But the people in the private houses took proper care of their animals. They had enough money to own cars and to make their homes look attractive.

I felt more cheerful when I walked past these houses – as if I had stepped into a nicer, cleaner, more positive world where things were possible rather than impossible. As I walked or cycled along, I imagined what it would be like to live in one of them. This was how my desire to leave Eastfield first began. I knew I didn't want to live on a council estate for the rest of my life. I knew I had to find a way out.

Chapter 7
Out of control

My final year at primary school came to a swift end in 1976 and I automatically transferred to Pindar School which served the council estate and surrounding areas. Sadly, it was rated as second from the bottom in the Scarborough area owing to the fact that aspirations on the estate were generally low. It was clear that what went on in people's homes had a direct impact on the school. There were schools with better performance levels within reach; however, Mum didn't look at any alternatives and, as was customary at that time, I simply went to the school that was nearest.

At this time I still spent much of my time outdoors. I had started saving all my pocket money at the age of ten, depositing it in a post office account. In my early teens I took seasonal cleaning and waitressing jobs at hotels and cafés. By the time I was 14 I had saved almost enough to fulfil a long-cherished dream. Seeing an advert in the local paper, 'Horses and ponies for sale', I believed this was the moment I had been waiting for. With quite a bit of help from Mum, I bought a young, barely schooled horse from a local dealer for £185. She was a cheap, neglected dapple grey filly called Silver, terribly thin with sores on her body.

She wasn't anything to look at and could barely drag herself around the dealer's yard as I took her for a short 'test ride'. Although she was in a shocking condition, I went ahead and paid the money for her because, to me, any horse was better than none.

Debbie, a school friend who lived on a farm in Irton village, kindly offered to let me keep Silver in one of her parents' fields free of charge. It was such a joy to see Silver break into a canter and kick up her heels joyfully at her new-found freedom as we turned her into the field to enjoy the rich spring grass. Debbie, who owned a pony, helped me to source a cheap second-hand saddle and bridle. I then used my weekly pocket money and summer wages to buy grooming brushes and other equine equipment. In those days there was less fuss over the care of animals, so even with my meagre earnings I managed to cover the basics.

However, I could not afford to pay for the stabling, food, hay and straw needed through the winter, so a lady from a nearby village offered to look after and ride Silver through the winter. I would then take her back in the spring, at which point she would be turned out into the fields to feed mainly on the grass.

Not being properly schooled, Silver was quite a slow, sometimes stubborn, ride. Nevertheless, I spent much of my time riding freely along the beaches, cliffs and country roads and pathways of the North Yorkshire coast, sometimes with a group of other horse-owning girls, but mostly alone.

Over time, Jill and Shirley, my primary school classmates, receded into the background as I began to make new friends at Pindar. I became part of a girls' foursome. When I first got to know them, at age 14, my hair was still long and straight, as it had always been, but now it had changed colour again and was dark brown. I had never made much of a fuss over my appearance and even in my early teens was fairly unselfconscious.

However, Pauline, who was very much the leader of our group, felt it was time for me to get with it and discard what at the time was an old-fashioned look. At first I resisted, but eventually peer pressure won the day, and before long I found myself at a salon having layers cut into my hair. With the encouragement of my new friends, I bought a pair of 'pegs'. These were tapered trousers with four six-centimetre folds vertically stitched from the waistband down, two on each side of the front zip. With this purchase and the haircut I quickly changed from being a horse-mad girl into a rather insecure 15-year-old adolescent overly conscious of my appearance.

Unlike my friends at primary school, my new friends all came from broken homes. None of us was shocked by the others' stories. Broken homes were the norm at Eastfield – just about every child I knew on the estate was missing a parent, usually his or her dad. All three of my friends smoked and encouraged me to do so too but, having seen Andrew become hooked at age 15, I was afraid of the health risks posed by cigarettes, so I refused to take even a trial puff.

It wasn't long after this that my interest in boys began, but my friends and I were not attracted to the boys at school, who we thought of as immature when compared to the 18- to 21-year-olds we had started to meet in town. I caused Mum a lot of worry when my friends and I habitually hung around the coffee shops in Scarborough town centre getting to know a number of male foreign students. They were in Scarborough mainly to learn English before going on to study for medical degrees, and came from Egypt, Jordan, Kuwait, the United Arab Emirates and Sierra Leone.

I began going out regularly to bars and nightclubs. Gone were the plain clothes. I was now wearing make-up, miniskirts, three-inch stiletto heels and a 'boob tube' – a piece of glittery, red, elasticated, strapless material which clung round my torso. Although underage, I followed the lead of others and, feeling grown up, placed my first order for an alcoholic drink.

Mum had finally installed a phone at home, and this became my line of contact with various boyfriends and through which I made arrangements to go out and meet them. Mum tried to put a stop to my nightclubbing habit by withholding money, but I simply stole whatever I needed from her purse. Worse still, along with my friends, I went into clothes shops intending to shoplift some garments to add to my wardrobe. Although I knew stealing was against the law, I was not especially troubled in my conscience, seeing it more as a dare than something criminal or immoral. With my friends, I practised techniques for hiding the stolen goods under my coat.

At home I came and went as I pleased. Even Pauline, who I considered to be the ringleader of our group, had to stick to certain rules when it came to being out late. I didn't have any such restraints because there wasn't much enforcement of rules at home. It wasn't long before I was out of control.

This led to some awkward situations. One evening I was walking down Scarborough's main street arm-in-arm with a Kuwaiti boyfriend when, out of the blue, Mum suddenly appeared to confront me. She had recently purchased a yellow moped with matching helmet. That evening she had parked the moped down a nearby street and was on foot, but was still wearing the helmet. Through the visor, in an angry, muffled voice, she ordered me to go home. I felt so utterly embarrassed and humiliated by her presence that, without a word, I turned on my stiletto heel and stormed off to catch a bus home. I had been feeling so grown up, strutting down the high street dressed to kill, only to be reminded that I was actually still a schoolgirl under parental care.

I was furious. When I arrived home, Mum was already there. I found her laying new lino on the toilet floor and flew at her in a rage, shouting, swearing, calling her names and punching her as hard as I could.

My lack of discipline eventually began to impact on my behaviour at school. With my three friends I began absenting myself from lessons. Immediately following the afternoon registration on a Wednesday, we would sneak round the back of the woodwork block and climb over the low wooden fence. Giggling with excitement, we then ran to the nearest bus stop to catch a bus into Scarborough, where we made for the coffee shop where our boyfriends hung out.

This went on for several weeks until another pupil 'grassed' on me – 'grass' was a word we used for being reported. Up until this point I had always been eager to please my teachers, so I felt mortified when they questioned me about my absenteeism. I was alarmed that I might start to be perceived as badly behaved. I didn't want to be seen that way and was furious with the pupil who had reported me. I was sure I knew who had informed the teacher about my misbehaviour and, seizing the opportunity after class, pursued her down the stairs. I then accosted her, grabbed her by the scruff of the neck and, swearing at her, delivered a hard kick to her shin.

In spite of wanting to maintain a good reputation, my behaviour continued to deteriorate. On one occasion I was due to play in a school concert. At age 14 I had started learning to play the viola and had joined the school orchestra. On the day of the concert, I had been entrusted with the music for the three viola players, of which I was one. I took it home to do some last-minute practice and was expected to return with it prior to the concert. However, it so happened that my friends were heading off to a nightclub that evening and asked whether I would like to join them. The temptation was too great, so instead of returning to school as expected, I went out for a night on the town, leaving my fellow viola players high and dry without their music.

Needless to say, the next day the music teacher responsible for the concert was bedside himself with anger and stopped me as I made my way to assembly. Within earshot of the entire school gathered in the hall, I was berated and told it was 'the lowest thing' I could possibly have done. I offered no apology, and instead rudely shoved my viola into his hands, swearing and telling him I no longer wanted to play it. I then turned and walked away.

Quite how it came about and why Mum agreed to it I cannot imagine, but I organised a party at my home, and my three friends and I invited some of our exotic boyfriends. Yet when the event came around there was insufficient space to dance in the front room, it was broad daylight and, in spite of the blaring stereo player, there was little party atmosphere as we all just sat around on the sofa and chairs. To crown it all, Mum had refused to leave the house and instead joined in the party, wafting in and out of the front room wearing a long, red kaftan and carrying plates of crispbread with cheese. I felt so humiliated by the fact that our boyfriends weren't impressed by the party or by our poor offerings of food, presented on plates on the hearthrug. I cringed as one of them contemptuously nudged the food away with his foot, and I regretted having ever decided to have a party.

Things began to take a serious turn when I started dating an Egyptian called Ismail. Mum was especially concerned about this friendship and, knowing that Ismail was soon to return to Egypt, she went to my school to express her worries to Mr Wallis, the deputy headmaster.

I learned later that, appearing initially rather surprised at hearing this, Mr Wallis eased his lanky frame out of his office chair, retrieved a file from his cabinet and flipped it open. After reading my reports for a minute or two he closed the file and, with a dismissive hand movement, replied, 'No, no, Mrs Webster, Amanda's *far* too sensible to do something like that.' Clearly, references to my absenteeism and the incident with the viola had not yet made their way into Mr Wallis' filing cabinet! Hesitating slightly, he continued, 'But if you are *still* concerned, I'm happy to drive you to Scarborough station on the day this man leaves.'

Then, feeling slightly embarrassed that she might have been causing a fuss over nothing, Mum said, 'No, it's fine. I'm sure you're right. I'm probably worrying about nothing.'

I had had no thoughts whatsoever of trying to elope to Egypt, but when it came to the day of Ismail's departure, that changed. Having nothing with me save the school uniform I was wearing, I announced to Ismail at the train station that I wanted to go with him to Egypt. The decision was completely unpremeditated and very sudden. Why I decided to do this was and still remains a mystery! Ismail was standing at the ticket kiosk about to pay for my train ticket to London when, suddenly and completely unexpectedly, Andrew roared up the station forecourt on his motorbike. Seconds later Mum arrived on her moped, and Span appeared, wearing a furry hat and horn-rimmed spectacles. She then strode over to Ismail and began to tell him off, angrily wagging her finger at him. Ismail responded by suggesting that *I* was the crazy one. Pauline had also come to the station to witness his departure and had been amazed by my sudden decision to join him. I felt so embarrassed by the presence of my family members that, without any more ado, I waved goodbye to Ismail and, to Mum's great relief, never saw or heard from him again.

Chapter 8
Life and death

Throughout my teens I didn't attend church, except for one occasion when Mum asked me to join her at the local Anglican service. We sat towards the front but I hadn't wanted to go and was bad-temperedly slumped in the pew, wearing a sullen expression. 'Go on, then. Impress me,' I thought as I critically observed the service, feeling bored by what I saw as 'a vicar droning on'.

As an adolescent, I believed Christianity was fake, a form of social control designed to keep people in a state of fear and obedience. I couldn't detect any relevance in it for my life, or for anybody else's for that matter. This attitude was no doubt compounded by the fact that our struggles appeared to go unrecognised by all of the local churches. No priest or congregation member tried to make contact with us and, likewise, except for the one visit, we kept our distance from them.

If anyone asked me what I believed when it came to spiritual matters, I usually replied that I thought reincarnation was likely. I had no particular reason to believe this, but it was convenient to have something to say if the subject of spirituality arose. I was also interested in astrology. I prided myself on being a Sagittarian and would often read through the qualities ascribed to my star sign, saying, 'Yes, that's me!' On one of his visits, Dad, having noticed my interest, bought me a mug with Sagittarius written on it and one with Cancer for Andrew. I also liked to guess what star sign other people might be, and often got it right. 'There must be something in it,' I told myself. I regularly consulted the star sign sections of teenage magazines, half-believing that events predicted for Sagittarians would come true in my life. However, I never took any practical steps or made decisions based on these predictions and mostly just forgot about them.

When it came down to it, as with most people of my age at the time, I had no reasoned answers to the big questions of life and death – nothing that I could depend on in an hour of need. This became clear when I almost lost my life on two occasions.

Before I owned Silver, I often spent time with a lady in her twenties called Cathy, who lived on the other side of the dell in an area known as Dale Edge, deemed to be the toughest part of the estate. Riding was her passion. She owned several ponies and a horse, which she kept on a farm in Cayton. It seemed every penny she owned was spent on maintaining these animals, and she prioritised them above everything else in her life. Even her house had been taken over as storage space for equine equipment.

I latched on to her, hoping for free rides. This happened quite often, and she would allow me and one or two other girls to ride the ponies while she rode the horse: Maverick, a handsome black gelding, standing at more than 15 hands high. I could see he was a lively ride but Cathy was able to handle him – and I desperately wanted to ride him too.

Then one winter afternoon, much to my surprise and delight, Cathy asked me to ride Maverick unaccompanied from her home back to the farm in Cayton, a ride of several miles involving traffic. I was 13 and I knew he was a large animal for me to handle, but what young teenager keen on riding would turn down an offer like that? Adding to the adventure, Maverick wasn't wearing a saddle. Instead Cathy had strapped on a New Zealand rug: a large, green canvas covering used for keeping a horse warm when kept outside in cold weather.

I was thrilled to be entrusted with such a fine horse. 'Wait till people see me now,' I told myself, proudly setting off from Dale Edge and heading down the dell. I planned to take Maverick for a steady canter along the length of the dell and turned his nose so that he was facing diagonally across and up its steep slope. We began at a leisurely pace but soon broke into a canter. I was feeling very grand.

Then suddenly, Maverick did something which completely took me by surprise. About halfway up the dell, knowing he was heading home, he tossed his head in the air, took the bit between his teeth and broke into a flat-out gallop. The diagonal distance from the bottom to the top of the dell was not very long, certainly not sufficient for a horse to safely gallop and slow down before reaching the road which ran along the top of the dell. We tore along, the edges of the New Zealand rug flapping wildly against Maverick's sides, the wind roaring in surges past my ears with each giant stride.

It was dusk and I wasn't able to see my surroundings very clearly. Up ahead through the dim light I could see car headlamps coming in the opposite direction to us along the top of the dell. Maverick wasn't responding to anything I did; his powerful neck was like iron as I fought with the grip he had on the bit. Frantically wondering what to do, I fleetingly glanced at the long grass and bushes rushing past in a blur on my left. 'Should I simply bail out by jumping off?' I thought. But I couldn't tell which would be more dangerous: to jump off at speed or to stay on the back of a bolting horse. In this terrifying moment I believed I was about to be killed. This was it. This was how my life would end, I told myself, suddenly strangely calm and detached at the thought. I would be the 13-year-old girl killed in a riding accident.

There was no more time to think. We had almost reached the road, and in front was a pair of headlamps penetrating the misty twilight. We were heading straight for an oncoming car.

What happened next was astonishing. I had thought that Maverick, having horse sense, would slow down once he got close to the road, but no, he maintained his speed and careered straight off the grassy kerbside and on to the road, just as the car was approaching.

Incredibly, such was the timing that, instead of smashing into the front or side of the car and ending up in a mangled mess of horse, metal and glass as I had expected, we shot behind the vehicle, missing it by inches.

Maverick, now on tarmac, slowed to a canter. I could feel the stares of one or two surprised pedestrians as his iron-shod hooves clattered loudly on the hard surface. He continued until we reached the bottom of the road and crossed over a roundabout. Only then did he come to a halt. By now I was in a state of total shock. Knees shaking,

I immediately slid off and, shouting at him, pummelled his rippling neck with my fist.

I felt embarrassed by the fact I had been unable to control my mount, so I shook off the irritating attentions of a concerned passer-by. I then slipped the reins over Maverick's neck and set off for the farm on foot, Maverick now quietly walking by my side. There was still some distance to go by road and I didn't want to risk a repeat incident. 'How did I emerge from this unscathed?' I kept asking myself.

Still feeling badly shaken as I walked Maverick home, I couldn't help but wonder at the narrow miss with the car. It had seemed almost miraculous. 'Was something or someone taking care of me?' I wondered.

Two years later, on a school exchange visit to Germany, I came close to losing my life again. I was standing with some other people waiting to cross the road. Whizzing past were not just cars, buses and lorries, but trams as well. I knew that the traffic in Germany travelled on the right-hand side of the road, not on the left as in the UK, but for some reason that had completely gone out of my mind.

Looking to the right, and thinking that the road was clear, I had only taken a couple of strides from the kerb when I heard shouting behind me. Wondering what the cacophony was about, I looked back. The people I had been standing with were still on the kerb, wide-eyed and calling out to me in German – I couldn't tell what. I still hadn't realised what the danger was but the expressions on their faces were enough to convince me I was in some kind of peril, so I turned right round and retraced my two steps – just in time – as I felt a strong whoosh of wind sweep over

91

the back of my head and neck. A tram had narrowly missed me.

These indicators of my own mortality didn't cause me to search seriously for answers to matters of life and death; yet, possibly subconsciously, they were stark reminders of the fragility of life, and contributed to my growing belief that I was being watched over. I would relate these near-death stories to friends, ending my tale with the thought that perhaps I was being looked after in some special but, at this time, undefined way.

Although I was all at sea when it came to spiritual matters, intuitively, perhaps, I had some sense of a deeper reality. It made sense to me that there was some sort of God somewhere, but I felt sure 'it' was only interested in very religious people such as Mother Teresa or the Pope. I believed any God who did exist must surely be the preserve of famous saints, the kind of people whose statues graced churches and cathedrals. He certainly wouldn't be interested in a teenager on a council estate. I believed I didn't come anywhere near being good enough for a God.

Whatever the truth of the matter was, I had no clear idea about it, and neither did my immediate family. Mum didn't have any close friends so, apart from Span, hardly anyone came to our house. However, the council estate was occasionally targeted by tarot card readers and, more often, by Jehovah's Witnesses and Mormons on recruitment missions. Mum's loneliness was such that she would allow anyone who knocked on the door into the house because their company was better than none.

I was as critical of these people as I was of Christianity and the institutional Church as a whole. I disliked them coming to our house because I felt their sole aim was to push their beliefs on to us. I recall one day when some Mormons approached our front door. I was standing in the garden and, as no one answered the door, they turned to leave, greeting me as they walked past. Fed up at yet another visit from them, I angrily blurted out, 'I want nothing to do with Joseph Smith and co!' (Joseph Smith was the founder of Mormonism.) Surprised by my aggressive tone, the mild-mannered Mormons didn't respond but slunk away down the garden path.

I couldn't put into words why, but I didn't think that either the Mormons or the Jehovah's Witnesses were propagating something authentic. At the time I rejected both mainstream Christianity and these other religious expressions, believing them to be human constructs. I was not prepared to accept any of them.

Mum seemed open to all comers when it came to spirituality. Occasionally she consulted fortune tellers of various types working on Scarborough seafront, and afterwards she would relate to me what they had told her. Alarmingly, some of it was even about me. I found it unnerving that someone sitting in a hut on Scarborough seafront, who had never met me, should claim to know my future. I had no knowledge of what the Christian Church and the Bible had to say about the occult, but I found it unnerving when Mum invited the tarot card readers into our front room. It bothered me that I had no knowledge of what they were doing and I was fearful of being influenced by spiritual forces which I couldn't even begin to understand. I felt safer having nothing to do with them, and when they sat down with Mum and pulled out their cards I would leave the room, marvelling at Mum's willingness to subject herself to ideas and forces I thought might well be evil.

However, one winter's evening when I was 15, there was no escape. I was with Pauline and Jez, another member of our foursome. At Jez's house, her mum decided to conduct a Ouija board session. I was surprised because, prior to this, I had had no idea she was involved with what I thought to be risky activities in the spiritual realm.

We were in the kitchen-diner, which was identical to the one at my house, except for a breakfast bar. I was sitting at the bar when the three of them asked me to participate in the Ouija board session. I declined, feeling as afraid of this as I had of the tarot cards. I insisted I wasn't interested and that they could go ahead without me. However, they kept pressurising me to join them, so reluctantly I agreed to do so and moved over to the table.

Jez's mum had placed cards showing letters of the alphabet in a circle on the kitchen table. I sat opposite her. Pauline and Jez were on either side. Then Jez's mum put a small glass in the middle of the table, inside the circle of cards. She instructed us each to suspend a finger over the top of the glass. Feeling very apprehensive I stretched out my right arm and obediently held my finger over the top of the glass as Jez's mum pronounced, 'If anyone's there, come in!'

Almost instantly I felt the air around the top of the glass turn ice cold. Mysteriously, the glass then began to move swiftly and purposefully across the table, pausing momentarily in front of one card before going to another. I watched open-mouthed as the glass spelt P-A-U-L-I.

Pauline suddenly let out a nervous laugh and the glass came to an abrupt halt.

Nothing more happened. I looked at Pauline, then at Jez's mum. What was the meaning of the phenomenon I had just witnessed? The session seemed to be over and, as Jez's mum began to gather up the cards, I sat in my seat dumbfounded. I waited until she had stood up and turned away, then, as inconspicuously as possible, had a thorough look at the underside of the table. I had expected to see a mechanism of some sort, levers or strings that Jez's mum might have set up earlier. But there was nothing of that kind to be seen.

That night I stepped out of Jez's house into the bitter cold and winter darkness. Walking down the garden path I glanced up at the night sky. It seemed darker than usual. I felt vulnerable and alone. What had I taken part in? Fearful that perhaps something, or someone, was watching me, I wrapped my coat tightly around my body, wanting to feel safe, and walked quickly through the night. Foremost in my thoughts was the fear that I had taken part in something evil.

Chapter 9
Father figure

Through my early and mid-teens Mum had three boyfriends. 'Potential stepfathers?' I wondered to myself. Yet Andrew and I had very strong opinions about any man who might assume that role. Our judgements were often scathing, and we didn't hold back from telling Mum what we thought. Invariably, Andrew and I would give the man in question an unflattering nickname derived from his physical attributes or a word association created by our imaginations.

One such was Philip. When he arrived at our house, I cringed as he put on a pair of slippers and planted a fatherly kiss on my cheek. 'A good show,' I thought, cynically. I took an instant dislike to him, quite certain he was too overweight to be Mum's boyfriend. When he referred to our shabby house as a 'palace' compared to where he lived, I thought perhaps he was only angling for a rent-free place to stay.

Then there was Adam, or 'Clown', as Andrew and I nicknamed him. It was the prominent lines around the corners of his mouth when he laughed that inspired this name. He was, however, better looking than Philip. He had a full head of blond hair and was slim and reasonably tall, but he seemed to have a weak personality. I thought he was altogether too effeminate, too feeble, to be our dad. As with Philip, it only took a barrage of negative comments from me and my brother in order for the hapless suitor to be shown the door.

The only promising prospect was Bryn. He came on the scene when I was 15. Bryn was an English engineer based in Mauritius whom Mum had met at a local dance. His exotic place of work immediately caused him to rise in the rankings of potential suitors, and the fact that he was tall, slim and had a well-paid job added significantly to the appeal. He was the only one Andrew and I approved of as a suitable match for Mum. I hoped she would marry him. But Mum's indecisiveness and her fears that once based in Mauritius I might later struggle to gain access to quality higher education meant it was not to be.

In the end, none of Mum's boyfriends was able to assume the role of father to me and Andrew. Neither Philip nor Adam were on the scene long enough to do so, and Bryn was, more often than not, thousands of miles away. There was, however, one person who became an important figure in our lives throughout our teenage years: Mum's brother, Uncle David.

After doing a three-year apprenticeship in electronics, Uncle David had moved south from Hornsea in his early twenties to work as an electrical officer on the *Queen Elizabeth II* cruise ship. He later worked for an electrical engineering firm, then became an award-winning salesman with a double glazing company. His reward included being granted a once-in-a-lifetime trip on Concorde. Recognising his own talents in later years, he set up his own double-glazing business, which was very successful.

To me and Andrew, and probably to Mum, Span and Gramps as well, Uncle David was an exciting person to have in the family. He was full of life, fun and adventure. Although he lived nearly 300 miles away in Southampton, he visited us several times a year throughout the time we lived with Mum in Eastfield, and always joined us for Christmas. Andrew and I were very excited by his visits. When Uncle David stepped through the front door of our house, the atmosphere changed. Here was someone with energy, enthusiasm, opinions and goals in life. Uncle David had a job, friends, his own house, one foreign girlfriend after another, and an active social life. His deep, loud voice boomed as he let rip with his opinions, and he could be heard all over the house. 'This country stinks!' he would rant, complaining about the amount of tax he had to pay as a business owner. 'I'm not staying here. I'm off to New Zealand!' Then the topic would change and there would come a roar of laughter – usually at someone else's expense. When Uncle David was around, there was never a dull moment.

In the early years of his visits he owned a series of old cars, and would arrive at our house in his latest acquisition. My favourite ones were a red soft-top MG and later a soft-top TR6, both sports cars, the rattling doors and windows held together with sealing wax and string. The cars, though small, had enough space behind the front seats for two excited children to squeeze into. Having a car to ride in was thrilling, and not just any cars – ones with open tops!

Unlike Dad, Uncle David loved the outdoors and, without fail, would take me, Andrew, Mum and our dog, Mick, on day trips across the North York Moors or the Yorkshire Dales. Here we would enjoy challenging walks across the wild and windy landscape, usually with a picnic halfway.

There was something about Uncle David that attracted high drama, and some of our fondest childhood memories were formed by the times we spent with him. He had a mischievous streak, and was always ready to play a practical joke. On one occasion in Goathland, on the North York Moors, Uncle David, Mum, Andrew and I, along with Mick the dog, had just enjoyed a long walk to Skelton Tower, an old ruin. On the way back we were followed by a large dapple grey horse, apparently turned loose to graze. It pursued us as we returned to the car, hoping for something to eat other than grass. Uncle David, Andrew and I all reached the car ahead of Mum, who then became the object of most interest to the horse which, noticing her thick head of hair, mistook it for hay and tried to take a mouthful. Seizing the moment, Uncle David started the car engine and, with me and Andrew in the back, and, laughing loudly, began to drive away. Mum called frantically to him to stop while she and Mick ran behind the car, with the horse bringing up the rear.

As the eight years I lived at Eastfield went by, Uncle David became a dad-substitute for me and Andrew. His natural sense of fun and enthusiasm for life were infectious. I wanted to be like him. I loved Span and Mum, but I didn't particularly want to emulate them because of their weak points. I wasn't convinced Mum was emotionally and psychologically strong and, frustratingly, Span never stood up to Gramps' domineering rule. I wanted to emulate someone strong, independent and capable, a person with drive and ambition and a sense of adventure – preferably with the means to travel and experience all that life had to offer. Uncle David had ambitions to move to the Antipodes, and often talked about it. As a result I also began to consider the possibility of living in a distant country when I grew up. My later love of travel was no doubt partly a result of these conversations in my teenage years about far-off places.

I needed someone to follow as an example and, although it was probably unknown to him, Uncle David became that person. On our walks I made a determined effort to keep up with his big strides and made a point of not complaining that the walk was too fast or too long. I wanted to impress him, and was often rewarded afterwards when he praised my efforts. Likewise, around the tea table in the evening I would eat as much as I could and then revel in my uncle's astonishment at the amount of food I could consume. Not having a father who praised me, I did anything I could to impress my uncle just so he would affirm me.

It didn't always work. On one of his visits he was shocked that Andrew and I had picked up some bad language from our neighbourhood. I had been trying to impress him by using the 'f' word, but he turned to Mum and said, 'By gum, Ann, these kids' language is a bit ropey.' Instantly I felt a wave of embarrassment flood over me, my face, neck and ears becoming hot and red. My attempt to impress my uncle had backfired. I was mortified and resolved never to swear in front of him again. His approval was very important to me. I wanted him to think well of me and this, along with my desire to escape from Eastfield, was what helped spur me on to achieve my goals.

Unlike Mum, Uncle David had no time for anything spiritual. Perhaps his dismissal contributed in part to my own cynical attitude towards religious belief at this time. Except for the one occasion I reluctantly went to church with Mum at Eastfield, attending Sunday services had stopped when I was aged six – at the time Ella had become my stepmother. So on Sundays Mum, Andrew and I would usually stay at home with nothing to do. It was my least favourite day of the week, when shops and places of entertainment were closed. I felt puzzled by Sunday. It seemed to be a pointless, empty kind of day in which I often felt gloomy and despondent. What was I supposed to do with this apparent 'non-day'? Although there were one or two churches within walking distance of our house, the thought of going to one of them simply never entered my head. They were, to my mind, irrelevant.

And yet there were times when I wondered about the existence of God. My bedroom window faced east, and on the rare mornings when the Yorkshire sky was clear, before going to school I would stand at my window and stare at the rising sun. The net curtains consisted of rows of oval holes large enough for me to hook my fingers through as I peered through them and the drips of condensation on the glass, watching as the morning sun's golden rays slowly burned their way between the chimneys and over the rooftops. In these moments I sensed something beyond the sunrise, a presence that something in me wanted to reach out to and touch. But these experiences were only momentary. The demands of the school day would begin, and my attention would be diverted by what I considered to be more pressing things.

Chapter 10
Andrew

Being just over two and a half years older than me, my brother Andrew was much more aware of what was happening when our family began to fall apart.

In every respect he was a healthy little boy, developing normally. He was, in my eyes, quite a good-looking child and, unlike me, had inherited Mum's colouring, with a fresh complexion. His light blond hair had a distinctive 'calf's lick' above his forehead which caused one half of his fringe to be permanently swept up, giving him a cheeky look. At age three he had an eye operation to correct his squint, and as a very young child he wore round, pink-framed glasses.

Over all the ever-changing years and moves from here to there, Andrew was always there, experiencing what I experienced, seeing and hearing the same things – like a quiet witness to what was happening to us both. I didn't know precisely how he was being affected by events – there was often so little to go on – but one day in the midst of the trauma he announced, 'I love my dad!' Another time he spoke of his disappointment about Mum's ongoing anxiety problems and told her, 'I prayed for you to get better, but you didn't.'

When we were living with Ella in Marton, Andrew and I shared his bedroom for a few months. My bed was positioned on the other side of the room from his, and often during the night I would hear him making an odd, champing sound. I lay awake trying to work out what it was. Only several years later did I realise he had been anxiously grinding his teeth as he slept. We were so emotionally neglected: no one explained anything to us, no one put their arms around us and reassured us that everything would be all right. The world appeared to be a sad, scary place where things happened beyond our control; we had no say in decisions made on our behalf.

Once we arrived at Eastfield, Andrew, aged 12, was enrolled at Pindar School, and there were no concerns about his health. Although the teachers at the school commented that he was 'a bit of a dreamer', often gazing out of the classroom window, seeming to be in his own world, this wasn't something they were overly concerned about. After all, he was a boy and would probably have much preferred running around outside to sitting in a classroom.

As with most children, both Andrew and I had a mischievous streak. We would sometimes lean out of his bedroom window with a peashooter, aiming the dried peas at our elderly neighbour as he pottered about in his front garden. The aim was to shoot the peas into the round tobacco holder at the end of the pipe which almost invariably protruded from his mouth, pulling his bulbous, wet lower lip downwards. Given that the tobacco burner was only a couple of centimetres in diameter and we were 10 to 15 metres away, it was no wonder we could never get the peas to hit their target. Instead, they would bounce off our neighbour's shoulders and head, causing him to emit a gruff 'gi' arr!' in protest.

At other times we tied string at head height between our hedge and the lamp post in front of our house to annoy passers-by. Well hidden behind the net curtains in my brother's bedroom, Andrew and I would burst into fits of laughter on seeing people's irritation.

Sibling rivalry inevitably caused us to fight and argue. I was often on the receiving end of one of his 'Chinese burns' as he painfully twisted the skin on my forearm, or his 'knuckledusters', when he would clench his fist, poking out one knuckle, which he used to punch me on the arm, leaving a bruise. In return I would punch him back or kick him hard on the shin.

Having the bigger bedroom at Eastfield, Andrew slept in a high old double bed which had belonged to Span. Its heavy, dark wooden headboard became the scene of Andrew's electrical creativity – quite impressive for a teenager. He fitted switches into square holes cut into the headboard and wired them up from the back using old telephone wires which he had found in a bin at the local telephone exchange. He rigged one of his switches up to an abandoned street lamp timer which in turn controlled various appliances in his room. In the end, his headboard was covered in switches which operated the appliances, such as a television set, stereo system, vacuum cleaner and lights. Some were timed to go off in the morning, waking him up for school.

When Andrew was 15 Dad bought him an air rifle, which took .22 millimetre pellets. This was used in the back garden with empty tin cans and a row of cardboard ducks I had made for target practice. The rifle gave Andrew and me many hours of fun and entertainment. Apparently no one stopped to think that it might be put to wrong use.

But Mum began receiving reports from Andrew's teachers that he was not turning up for school. It came to light that he was 'skiving off', an expression used at Eastfield for being absent without permission. He and a friend were taking his air rifle and secretly spending time on the mud track which led to Oliver's Mount, shooting at cows and birds.

People tried to put a stop to Andrew's absenteeism, but over the next few months his wanderings along the Mount path during school time became a regular habit. Mum, Span, Gramps, Uncle David, the teachers and I watched helplessly as he left school at age 16 without any qualifications.

He increased his visits to the pub and would usually arrive home by ten o'clock. But, inevitably, one night ten o'clock came and went and Andrew did not appear. I went to bed as usual. I had school the next day but lay wide awake, aware he had not come home. Mum was downstairs, also waiting. I watched the clock as 10.30 came, 10.45, 11.00, 11.30. By now I knew there was a problem. I lay tense and restless, worried about my brother and his whereabouts.

At about quarter to midnight there was a loud knock at the front door. Mum, still awake downstairs, answered the knock. I crept to the bottom of my bed to listen, straining my ears to hear what was being said. I heard a man's voice and my brother's name mentioned. It was the police.

Andrew and an accomplice had been arrested after breaking into a pub in Cayton and stealing several crates of beer, and were being held at the police station. My heart sank. This was another indication that Andrew's life was spiralling out of control. He and his accomplice were required to attend court and were each fined £75.

Mum could exercise little parental control over Andrew. One afternoon, during one of our fights, Andrew had hit me particularly hard. At the end of her tether, Mum picked up my riding whip, strode into the lounge and, with all her strength, brought it down hard on Andrew's back as he sat forward on the sofa drinking tea from a mug. Being whipped in this way was such a shock that he responded by hurling the mug straight at Mum, shouting insults. The mug broke on impact as it hit Mum's elbow, causing a deep gash. Frightened, I ran to fetch a tea towel from the kitchen to stem the bleeding. I felt shaken by this violence in our family and couldn't bear the fact that my brother, whom I cared about, had badly injured someone else I loved.

Shortly after leaving school, Andrew took a casual job at a holiday camp further down the coast. He used his wages to buy a second-hand Honda SS50 motorbike. I admired the way he taught himself to dismantle then reassemble the entire machine. However, there was no resident father figure or mentor in his life to guide and encourage him in this interest so, sadly, it didn't develop beyond his tinkering with the motorbike in our back garden.

Then, when Andrew was 19, something happened which was so terrible I didn't want to accept it. He was taking part in a Youth Opportunity Programme at a local electrical firm, but the scheme was badly structured and he didn't benefit from it. Sadly, for reasons unknown to me, his application to work there as an apprentice failed. He felt depressed and began to believe that people could read his thoughts. His doctor prescribed an antidepressant. This was the beginning of much distress in our family as Andrew embarked on a life dependent on prescription drugs.

His initial feelings of paranoia deepened into a psychosis as his health deteriorated. One morning, after another late night at the pub, he told me he had seen a box behind the bar move without anyone touching it. Feeling quite alarmed, I responded by saying he must have imagined it. Inanimate objects didn't just move on their own, I reasoned with him. I closed the subject but felt unnerved. Why had Andrew said such a strange thing?

Dad's six-monthly visits continued throughout this time. It was now becoming clear, even to him, that Andrew was going down a road that was of concern to all of us. On one of his visits, Dad looked at Mum and, pointing first at me and then at my brother, said: '*She'll* be all right; it's *him* I'm worried about.'

Andrew's interest in motorbikes continued as he replaced one for another, ending up with a Honda H100. Having left the Youth Opportunity Programme at the electrical firm, and with no offer of further training, he took another job at the holiday camp, working in various roles including calling bingo numbers in an entertainment arcade and serving customers at cash kiosks. Throughout, his health continued to deteriorate.

One morning he described what had happened when he had been watching TV the night before. In those days transmission terminated at midnight and the picture became a fuzzy haze of black and white dots. Andrew told me that he had been staring at the screen after midnight and had seen two rows of crucifixes, one on the right and the other on the left, and was convinced he was moving through the middle.

Sometimes, late at night when we were all in bed, I would hear him laughing hysterically in his bedroom, a high-pitched laugh, nothing like his normal laughter. It didn't sound like him at all. It would continue for some time and was frightening. I couldn't understand what was happening to him. When I heard the laughter I froze in my bed, unable to move. Neither Mum nor I stirred while this was happening. By now we knew something was seriously wrong with Andrew but we had no diagnosis or way of dealing with it. The doctors continued to prescribe a range of antidepressants and anti-psychotic drugs, but it was unclear whether any of these actually helped.

Andrew eventually gave up his holiday camp job, as he was unable to sustain it owing to his illness. As the days went by, he began to report more hallucinatory experiences, both visual and audible. He rarely divulged how he felt about his life. However, one day we were both sitting at the kitchen table. Andrew was eating a hard-boiled egg with toast when suddenly he burst into tears. I had not seen him cry for years, and I felt surprised. Holding his head in his hands he sobbed, 'There's no future.' I tried to calm him and reassure him there was, but deep down I was equally fearful and uncertain.

His regular visits to the pub continued, and after he arrived home one night I could tell he had drunk too much. I was standing in the semi-dark in the back spot after doing some maintenance to my bike when Andrew suddenly appeared in the doorway. The light of the kitchen shone behind his tall, dark silhouette as he approached me and, completely unexpectedly, produced a small blade. I recognised it as the red-handled Stanley knife we had used for trimming our ill-fitting carpets. Holding it up to my face, he said in a threatening voice, 'I'm gonna kill ya.'

The wall was behind me and my bike was to my right, preventing me from backing away. This was so out of character that I instantly believed he was under some kind of influence and could be expected to carry out his threat. I stiffened and looked at the knife, which was a few centimetres away. One swipe and he could scar my face for life or slash my jugular vein. Without saying a word, I slowly stepped to the left and walked around him into the kitchen, hoping he wouldn't follow me. He didn't.

That night I pulled the end of my bed halfway across my bedroom door so no one could open it. What if he tried to attack me while I was asleep? This incident was so unlike Andrew that I found it hard to accept, let alone interpret. He was generally passive, even gentle, and would not usually look for trouble. I wondered what could have caused him to behave in that way. Was it just alcohol, or were there other influences in his life which none of us knew about?

Then Mum told me that one night while I was staying with a friend, she had heard a lot of crashing and banging downstairs as she lay in bed in the early hours of the morning. Before she had gone to bed, Andrew had threatened her with a carving knife in the kitchen, lifting it high above her head, as if preparing to strike. Her remarkably calm response had been to say sternly, 'Put that down!' – an instruction he had thankfully obeyed. However, now fearing that her life might be in danger, she had crept downstairs in the dark, pulled on her coat and slipped out. Half-running, half-walking, she had made her way through the night to Span's house. The frightening reality was that she had no idea what damage her son might be doing to the house – or worse, what harm he could be doing to himself. It had been two o'clock in the morning.

Shortly after this, in 1981, a very concerned Uncle David stepped in and invited Andrew to stay at his home in Southampton. Uncle David was now in a steady relationship with an Australian lady, and it was hoped that between them they would be able to help Andrew make a fresh start. Sadly, in spite of their efforts over the course of six months, Andrew's life did not improve. He was found collapsed in the street one night after drinking too much and was taken to Southampton Hospital. Following this incident, Uncle David and his lady friend felt there wasn't much more they could do, so Andrew returned to live at Eastfield.

One day while riding his motorbike, he fell off, breaking his ankle. This resulted in a hospital stay, after which he was transferred back home. His leg, from his ankle to his thigh, was encased in plaster, and he relied on crutches to move around the house. At this time his mental state went into further decline.

A year later he left home again to work for a travelling circus, but after several months he quit this job and returned home. Eventually he moved out altogether and rented a flat while living on benefits. His unstable mental state meant employment was out of the question.

On entering his twenties, it was clear that Andrew's illness was not going to go away. As general practitioners and psychiatrists became increasingly involved, he was diagnosed as schizophrenic. None of us wanted to accept it, thinking it was perhaps just a strange phase. How could a normal young man suddenly, and without any obvious explanation, become a mental health patient? All of us – Span, Gramps, Uncle David, Mum and I – were all in a state of shock and denial. Sadly, I had no idea what Dad thought about it.

Chapter 11
Big questions

I was 16, and my time at Pindar School finally came to an end in 1981, something I was very glad about. It wasn't that I had disliked the school or been unhappy there, but leaving was a significant marker in my quest to escape from the estate. I also had a nagging feeling that over the five years I hadn't learned very much, the teachers having often struggled to maintain classroom control.

On the very last day I placed my school uniform and exercise books, which had been so important in revising for my O Levels, in a pile on the vegetable patch where I had sometimes grown carrots and potatoes. I then set fire to them. Standing back, I watched wistfully as a chapter of my life went up in flames. It was my way of marking the end of an era and looking forward to the beginning of another. My efforts to get away from the estate and from Scarborough had advanced by a sizeable notch, and I was eager to move on to the next stage.

Once enrolled as an A Level student at Scarborough Sixth Form College, I found I had less to do with the friends I had made at Pindar School. The college, which was significantly smaller than the school, was situated around seven miles away from Eastfield in a fairly affluent area of

Scarborough, where grand Victorian houses stood on tree-lined streets.

I was allocated a place in Mr Doyle's class. He was a German specialist, a former Oxbridge graduate and a very conscientious and thorough teacher, attending to the finest points of grammar and pronunciation. He appeared to be middle-aged, was about my height and of slim build. He had a shock of wiry, greying hair around the sides and back of his head, the top being bald. He had fine features and wore glasses, but the most striking aspect of his appearance were his twinkly blue eyes, which accompanied his ready smile and lively sense of humour.

The classroom was about half the size of those at Pindar and the chairs were arranged in two concentric horseshoes, allowing us to look at one another during class. I didn't know any of the other students.

On the first day we chose our seats and I picked one near the window, close to Mr Doyle's desk. Next to me was a girl called Joanna, to whom I took an instant dislike. She had dead straight, mid-blonde hair which reached to just below her ears, with a fringe, and she had strikingly large blue eyes. 'What a toff,' I told myself as I looked at her round glasses and neatly trimmed hair and noted her 'posh' accent. Still, I decided to give her the benefit of the doubt and offered to share a locker with her, to which she replied with an instant and decisive, 'No.' It was much later that I discovered she had taken an instant dislike to me as well, having the immediate impression that I was cold and aloof.

Our timetable included General Studies, a range of academic disciplines from which we could choose. One of my chosen disciplines was Philosophy. By now I was, possibly at a subconscious level, seeking answers to the meaning of life. I was gradually being drawn into deep discussions about the nature of human beings, whether there was an ultimate purpose to existence – big questions which began to fascinate me. I had already reached the conclusion that people were intrinsically selfish and that everything they did was ultimately driven by the desire to promote their own interests. I would often talk about this with my friends, wanting to explore these ideas.

The Philosophy lessons were thoroughly enjoyable. I loved the bigger-picture thinking and found the subject very thought-provoking and stimulating. I didn't come away with any final conclusions or definitive answers, but these classes set me on a track of wanting to know more, to find answers. Who was I? Was there a purpose and value to my life? Something in me desperately needed to get to the bottom of such apparent mysteries.

On a college trip I had the opportunity to get to know Joanna better. We were on the back seat of the coach and had just set off when, to my great surprise, she pulled out a cigarette and started smoking. Having previously decided she was bound to be boring, this was a revelation. Her mischievous talk and behaviour led to one belly-laugh after another throughout the journey. I discovered that Joanna had a similar sense of humour to mine, and from that day we became firm friends, meeting every break at a corridor window which looked on to a tall pine tree. From this we affectionately nicknamed our meetings as 'Pine' and created a series of interchangeable nicknames for one another: Crump, Owl, Koala and Bean.

I learned that Joanna also came from a broken home and that her German mother had married for the third time. The third husband was a man of quite some means and, as a result, Joanna lived in a very nice, private, detached house in a village a few miles outside of Scarborough. Although her early background and financial circumstances were not dissimilar to mine, her current situation was very different.

During our two years in sixth form, Joanna sometimes invited me to her home, where she lived with her younger half-sister, her stepfather and her mum. I felt too ashamed to invite her to my house on the council estate. What would she think of me if she saw where I lived? I compared the expensive-looking furnishings in her house with our social services cast-offs. I looked at the bright, modern kitchen and thought about our drab kitchen-diner and grubby little back spot. Her well-tended gardens to front and rear showed up the paltriness of my own attempts to make our gardens look presentable. Joanna's family had two cars. Her mum wore make-up and smart, expensive-looking clothes. I compared her with my mum who, although still a very good-looking woman, wore plainer clothes and was still riding around on her yellow moped wearing the matching helmet.

Money made a big difference, and I couldn't compete. It was safer never to let Joanna anywhere near my house, so during the two years I never once invited her to my home. I would manipulate any situation where there was a risk she might come for a visit, thereby defusing any such suggestion.

I was completely mortified when, on one occasion, I failed to avoid being given a lift home in her mum's car.

'Is that your house?' Joanna asked me when we pulled up outside our shabby-looking council house.

'Yeah,' I replied almost under my breath, not wanting to admit that this was where I lived and keen to get this embarrassing moment over and done with as quickly as possible. Then, without another word, and avoiding Joanna's gaze, I quickly closed the car door and shot down the passage at the side of our house, thinking nonsensically that if I went up the passage instead of through the front garden gate she might think it wasn't where I lived. I didn't want Joanna to linger. I didn't want her to take in the environment. I wanted this moment to end as quickly as possible. I felt so ashamed. She never once spoke to me about my home after this, something for which I was very thankful.

In spite of the difference in our material circumstances, our friendship thrived, and it proved to be a help to me as I struggled through the difficulties my little family was facing.

It was during the summer holiday of 1982, when I was halfway through my A Levels, that Andrew had his motorbike accident. The plaster cast meant he spent most of his time lying on the lounge sofa in his pyjamas. At the same time he was gradually slipping into a deeper psychotic state and barely knew where he was.

Once again he began relaying details of visual and auditory hallucinations. I found these disclosures very distressing and wouldn't accept what was happening to him. I tried to counter what he was telling me with logical arguments, believing I could talk him out of it. But it didn't work, and as he went deeper into his psychosis he stopped eating. I began taking sandwiches to him as he lay in the lounge, trying to persuade him to eat while at the same time telling him that his thoughts made no sense. This situation continued day after day and I marvelled at Mum's capacity to persevere under the strain of these terrible circumstances. Yet she did, making her daily shopping trip to bring food back to the house and doing her best to keep things going.

As it was the long summer holiday of 1982, I was also at home most of the time and therefore witnessed Andrew's deteriorating condition on a daily basis. Over time this began to affect me and I found myself becoming quite stressed. Since he had fallen ill I had always feared that I too would be struck down in a similar way, and this almost became a self-fulfilling prophecy. I began to feel very uneasy and worked myself up into a panic. Feeling frightened, I confided in Mum that I thought I too might be going mad, to which she replied curtly, 'Well, you'd better go to the doctor, then.' I winced at her abrupt tone which made it sound as if she didn't care, but by now I knew that it was her way of coping with the terrible shocks she had absorbed over the years. She would have an emotional meltdown later in the day.

Not being one to rush to a doctor, I nevertheless made an appointment to see our family GP. I felt very anxious as I sat in front of the doctor in the consulting room. I told him how I was feeling and that, having seen what had happened to Andrew, I was worried I might end up the same. The doctor calmly looked at me and said, 'If there were really anything wrong, you wouldn't be sitting here like this telling me.'

I listened, unconvinced.

'But if you think it might help,' the doctor continued, 'I can prescribe you a tranquiliser just to get you through this rough patch.'

Believing that he must know best, I reluctantly agreed.

With feelings of trepidation I watched as the doctor wrote out a prescription, signed it with a flourish and handed it to me. This was the path both Mum and Andrew had gone down, and now I appeared to be heading the same way. It was the moment I had dreaded. I had so wanted to succeed, to never fail or be a victim, yet here I was, admitting defeat.

'This must be the beginning of the end,' I thought, my mind going straight to worst-case scenario as I stood up to exit the surgery.

Yet, even in my desperation, I grasped at the fact that I still had the power to make my own decision. I didn't *have* to follow the doctor's suggestion. Would I turn left, cross the road and go to the local parade of shops to pick up the medication? Or would I turn right and walk home without it? How would I then cope, having to face such unbearable circumstances at home? What was the right thing to do?

Then, as I walked through the garden at the front of the surgery and onto the public footpath, it happened. Something within me reached far back into the past, to the time I had sat on my bed as a young child, scowling at Ella, promising myself I would not be defeated, that I would never be a victim, that I would survive. I knew I didn't want to go down the road of dependence on prescription drugs. I wanted to succeed. I wanted to fight whatever I was feeling – and win. Veering to the right I walked slowly, lost in thought, hesitating, unsure.

Then the decision was made. Blocking any more doubts, I tore the prescription into bits, strode to a nearby bin and threw the pieces away. I then walked home and packed a suitcase.

Chapter 12
Making good my escape

I became increasingly aware that my developing friendship with Joanna was something of a godsend. I wanted and probably needed to get away from the stressful circumstances at home, so going to stay at her house for the rest of the summer holidays seemed to be the best thing to do. I even took Silver with me, as a local farmer had offered to let her stay in a small paddock not far from Joanna's house.

As far as Joanna knew, I had asked to stay at her house because I was worried about my brother. I had suddenly lost weight because I was now more concerned about myself than about Andrew – but I wasn't about to tell Joanna that. My vulnerability was still firmly locked behind a defensive wall. I didn't tell any of my friends about the emotional turmoil I was experiencing, and thankfully I didn't have to, as I rapidly began to feel better. Staying with Joanna turned out to be the best thing I could have done.

Later, reading a medical leaflet, I realised I had been suffering from stress at the time I had consulted my GP. It came as a great relief to discover it wasn't anything worse, and before long I returned home in time for the start of the academic year at the sixth form college. Once I was back in the sanity of the school environment in the autumn of 1982, any feelings of stress further evaporated. In addition, I was greatly helped by the fact that Andrew was no longer at home but was moving from place to place working for a travelling circus. As a result, the atmosphere became more relaxed, enabling me to focus on my studies.

Although no one in my immediate family had studied at university, I believed obtaining a place at a tertiary education institution was the best way to escape my current circumstances and leave Eastfield forever. Sadly, there had been a lack of aspiration among many of the pupils at Pindar School, and university studies were not regarded as an obvious goal. But for me personally, it was almost a matter of life and death, as I saw no future for myself in Scarborough. To achieve this, I went all out to get the A Level exam grades I so desperately needed.

Mum bought me a small, old-fashioned, wooden school desk, complete with an inkwell hole in its top right-hand corner. To improve its appearance I painted it bright yellow. Life became a strict routine of cycling to and from college, eating a meal Mum had prepared, then going straight upstairs to study. Often Mum and I would sit in the front room as she tested me on long lists of German vocabulary and quotations from English literature. This intense study went on relentlessly throughout the second year of A Levels, to the extent that I had to sacrifice much of the time I usually spent with Silver, so Mum took over the daily grooming duties.

Dad's six-monthly visits continued. He had never been a strong advocate of higher education, believing the best

124

way forward for a 16-year-old was to find a job and work one's way up, as he had done. In spite of his views, however, his reaction to my study plans seemed, overall, rather positive. 'So you want to be a professor, do you?' he asked me in his businesslike way during his December visit. Feeling nonplussed by the question I made no reply but simply looked at him. As I did so, I noticed him purse his lips together and nod his head slightly. Then, with a steely glint in his eyes, he said, 'Good stock.' A picture of cattle passed through my mind but I interpreted it as his way of saying he was pleased with my efforts; he just couldn't say so. The nearest he came to it was with his suggestion that it was presumably because of *his* genes that I had made it this far. No mention was made of Mum's commitment to education and all the sacrifices she had made for the family over the years.

During the second year of A Levels I became aware that Mr Doyle ran a group called the 'Christian Union' at the college. It was the first time I had heard of it and I had no clear idea what purpose it served. Mr Doyle made no direct mention of it in class, but by now I had an inkling that he was religious, although I had not heard him use the words 'Christian', 'Jesus' or 'church'. Instead, from time to time I would be struck by a casual comment he might make. For example, once, referring to a date far in the future, he speculated as to where he might be and then answered his own question with, '*Unter der Erde*', implying he would be dead and buried. He then laughed, his eyes twinkling. 'How on earth could he appear so cheerful at the thought of his own death?' I wondered. This intrigued me, but there was no immediate or obvious answer to my question.

At one point during my second year of A Level studies I had a bout of German measles. Being infectious, I had to stay away from the college until I had recovered. But I felt fit and well enough to keep cycling to the farm to see Silver, and occasionally go for a ride.

One afternoon during this time I heard a knock at the front door. I opened it and, to my great surprise and embarrassment, there was Mr Doyle, smiling and holding out some papers. I stared, momentarily lost for words and mortified that he could now see where I lived. I hadn't wanted anyone at the college to see. Soon everyone would know I lived on a scruffy council estate – or so I believed. But this wasn't an issue for Mr Doyle who, in his usual cheerful manner, told me he had brought me some homework so that I wouldn't fall behind with my studies. I was amazed. Mr Doyle, who always rode his bike to and from the college, had cycled all the way to my house, which was at least a seven-mile journey, up and down hills – just to give me a few papers. I couldn't fathom it. Why would he go to such trouble over *me*?

Once recovered from the measles, I returned to college and continued to study hard. Obtaining a place at university was now my dream. But where would I go? Which university should I choose?

Each student wanting to go into higher education was supplied with a slim, purple UCCA (Universities Central Council for Admissions) handbook which contained basic facts and details about all the higher education institutions available to us. While I was thumbing through the booklet, a name caught my eye: University of St Andrews. I had never heard of it nor did I know where it was, yet I was immediately drawn to it because of its name. There was something about the word 'saint' in St Andrews that I found attractive. I looked at the details and saw it was situated in Fife, on the east coast of Scotland. This was a strong plus point for me, not only was it coastal but it was also far away. I had not been to Scotland. I knew practically nothing about the country or, indeed, about the University of St Andrews. Yet, after reading more about the university and its location, I decided to apply. In a short space of time it became my all-consuming passion to get there – no other tertiary institution would do. I slept with the prospectus under my pillow. Although I never prayed, it was my way of expressing my longing, as if appealing to a higher force, perhaps fate, to make it possible.

It was the summer of 1983. I was 18 years old with two black eyes from a bad cycling accident the week before, and was on my bike making my way to the college to pick up my A Level results. The black eyes didn't matter now as I approached the college to see where my future lay. I knew what grades I needed to take up the offer of a place at St Andrews. Had all the hard work paid off?

As I went up the steps to the main entrance I bumped into Miss Sinclair, one of my two English Literature teachers who, grinning broadly, said, 'Good English result!' I felt my hopes rise but was worried that she hadn't mentioned my other grades – would they be good enough? I was about to find out. Taking what felt like the walk of my life, I hurried along the corridor to the noticeboard where all the students' grades had been posted. With butterflies in my stomach and my heart racing I stood alongside some others looking at their results. Then with my finger I traced horizontally from my name to the grades.

My heart leaped as I took in the news. I had made it! Filled with excitement and energy, and suppressing a scream, I tore back along the corridor to the college payphone. Barely able to stand still, I quickly dialled our home number. Within two rings Mum answered, and I pushed in a ten-pence piece. Without any introduction I cried, 'I made it!'

'I'll give you everything I've got!' she blurted back.

What a moment it was! A large door of opportunity had suddenly swung open. The future, once so fearful and uncertain, now seemed to hold the most wonderful promise. At *last* Mum and I had something to celebrate.

Now I would be leaving for Scotland, I sadly had to sell Silver. It was painful, but I had no choice because I needed the money to buy things for my new student life, including a large suitcase, clothes and bath towels. The rest of the money was to be kept as savings. As was my habit, I had taken a couple of summer jobs at a hotel and a café to earn cash.

It wasn't long after getting my exam results that Dad was due to come and see us. Andrew was now back at home after his time working for the travelling circus had come to an end.

As the day of Dad's visit approached, I began to feel slightly apprehensive. Now, aged 18, I barely knew him. The teenage years were drawing to a close and I had seen him perhaps 15 times since we had been sent to live with

Mum. He had become a stranger to me. Who was he as a person? What should I say to him?

It wasn't at all premeditated on my part, but when the time came I felt I couldn't face seeing Dad. Perhaps he had become such a remote figure in my life I no longer saw any value in spending time with him. That, combined no doubt with teenage self-centredness, caused me on the day of his visit to stay away at work. I carried on with my day, untroubled by the fact I had deliberately absented myself.

I returned home after work to find Dad had already left. Andrew had been at home and told me as soon as I walked through the kitchen door that Dad had instructed him to say, 'You can tell Mandy she's no longer my daughter.'

Something inside me seemed to break with the shock of these words. Absorbing the blow, I looked at Andrew, momentarily speechless. 'Surely he's not serious,' I thought, and waved my arm dismissively, saying, 'Aw, come on, what are you talking about?'

I hadn't stayed away out of malice but out of confusion and teenage awkwardness. I hadn't seen it as a big deal, but clearly Dad had. After the shock, I told myself that he hadn't really meant it – it was just an angry reaction to my absence. Had I known what I now know, that Dad had taken my absence very much to heart, I might have reacted very differently and taken immediate and positive steps to clarify things and re-establish our relationship. It was only over time that I would come to realise his intention. Right there and then I didn't have the benefit of hindsight. Life therefore went on, and it was only as the future began to unfold, as my attempts to make contact with Dad by letter were, to my great incredulity, met with silence, that it became very clear he had meant every word. I was indeed no longer his daughter. He had finally forsaken me.

Chapter 13
In search of the ancient paths

It was 1983 and Margaret Thatcher was Prime Minister. Although I had no interest in politics, I was grateful for a full government grant to cover all my expenses for the four-year degree programme I was embarking on.

I had never been a passenger on one of the high-speed InterCity 125 trains which served the length of the country, but here I was, boarding one with my big, new, blue suitcase and my bike, which I thought would be useful for student life. My case contained practically everything I owned. Only a couple of cherished toys, including the large golden-yellow teddy bear, had survived my teenage years, and these remained, neglected, in my little box-bedroom at Eastfield.

Arriving at Edinburgh Waverley train station, I couldn't make sense of the station master's strong accent as he shouted instructions up and down the platform. One thing was for sure: I was no longer in England! In Edinburgh I had to change platform and catch a train to Leuchars, the closest station to St Andrews. It turned out to be a Royal Air Force base and appeared to be in the middle of nowhere. There wasn't much to see from the train station, except a few bungalows some distance away.

I had been advised by the university to take a taxi from Leuchars station to St Andrews, which was a seven-mile drive, so I loaded my bike and suitcase into a large taxi and, together with another student, set off. The road wound this way and that as I sat in the back feeling tense and excited. 'What will my new life be like?' I wondered as we zigzagged along. Soon the landscape became windswept and coastal, broken by fir trees which occasionally blocked my view, casting shadows over the road and breaking the sun's rays, causing them to twinkle, diamond-like, through the trees' branches.

Unexpectedly, as we rounded a curve in the road, I saw a sight which took my breath away. In the distance I could see a small, grey town hugging the coastline, its silhouette made distinctive by a variety of spires and towers. Even from this distance I was enthralled by the powerful drive of the sea landwards. Its white-topped waves drove relentlessly towards the shoreline, sending a continuous spray into the air, which the wind picked up and blew across the town. Even though I had grown up by the sea, I had never seen such a striking seascape. Here was something ancient, something unique. This was St Andrews; I had arrived.

I had read that the university was the third oldest tertiary institution in the English-speaking world, after Oxford and Cambridge, but it was only as we drove around the narrow streets that I began to appreciate the full significance of this. The majestic, if slightly austere, grey stone buildings and narrow cobbled streets around the central marketplace were such a far cry from Eastfield.

I was eager to make the most of university life which, while sitting at my little yellow desk, I had worked hard to gain access to. During my first week I explored the Freshers' Fair, a big exhibition of all the activities available at the university. I was keen to see what was on offer and eagerly rushed around, astonished by the fascinating array of clubs, including the sublime – 'Dead Poet's Society' – and the ridiculous – 'Tunnock's Caramel Wafer Appreciation Society'.

The Freshers' Fair was housed in the new purpose-built Student Union building, its appearance a contrast to the old and architecturally interesting buildings which housed many of the university departments. I went up a flight of stairs to a broad walkway with open doors either side. Without conscious decision my feet turned sharply to the right and I found myself at the Christian Union exhibition. Curious at what was on offer, I recognised, if only from its name, that this club was 'religious'.

The Scottish university system was somewhat different to the English, and I was required to choose three subjects in the first and second years of a four-year degree. So I chose Philosophy as one of the three. The Philosophy classes at the sixth form college had whetted my appetite for more, and as I still did not have clear answers to my big questions, I thought it made sense to carry on with the subject.

I learned that the university had an 'academic parent' scheme whereby two third-year students – one male, the other female – would 'adopt' a first-year student, help them to settle in and deal with any concerns they might have throughout their first year. It was left to the students to choose whom they would 'adopt', and I had no idea who my 'parents' would be.

During the first week I was sitting in the Student Union bar with some other first years when a male student, holding a pint of beer, approached me and began chatting. He told me his name was Mark and he was a third-year Psychology student. He was tall and good-looking with thick, mid-brown hair which had started to recede at the hairline. During the course of our conversation he offered to be my academic father, so I accepted, pleased to have one more aspect of my settling in sorted out.

As the days went by, Mark made a point of visiting me, helping me to find my way around. He appeared to be a very conscientious academic father. One evening, as I was standing with him outside the Student Union preparing to cycle back to my room, he told me he had broken up with his girlfriend that very week, and would I be interested in being his girlfriend in addition to being his academic daughter?

I was taken by surprise and wasn't sure how to respond. I was impressed by the fact he had been honourable enough to put an end to things with his girlfriend before venturing to ask me, but the last thing I wanted at this stage of my life was another boyfriend. I had even opted to live in an all-female hall of residence just so I wouldn't come into too much contact with men. I had washed my hands of my teenage lifestyle of dating one boyfriend after another, and was determined that my new life at university would be associated with more worthwhile pursuits. Furthermore I didn't readily relate to Mark in that way and, naturally enough, needed time to think.

I learned much later that the attraction for Mark had been mostly because of our differences in background. He came from a very middle-class family who lived on the outskirts of Bath in a large, detached house surrounded by its own spacious, well-tended garden. His father was a medical doctor, his mother a music teacher. As a student, Mark even owned a car, a red Volkswagen Beetle. He disclosed that he found me unusual, even 'exotic', and was quite amazed, given my background, that I had been offered a place at one of the country's choicest universities. In spite of this, he had his misgivings. It transpired that Mark was a Christian who believed he should only date a girl who shared his faith. He admitted later that he knew I wasn't a Christian because my speech was peppered with the 'f' word. I, on the other hand, wasn't aware of my swearing – or of his dilemma.

While I was still wondering whether or not to be his girlfriend, Mark invited me to a Christian Union meeting, and I happily accepted. I was curious and wide open to ideas. He could have invited me to any spiritual, religious or philosophical gathering and I would have gone just as readily. The meeting was attended by around 100 students and Mark and I sat towards the back. The speaker talked at length but, although I could hear his words, they didn't convey anything to me; I couldn't understand what he was talking about.

My openness to spiritual things must have been apparent to Mark: on another occasion, while in my room, he asked me whether I would like to commit my life to following Jesus. I wasn't sure what this meant but was eager to try out anything religious or spiritual. After all, it was the spiritual suggestion in the name St Andrews which had attracted me to this university in the first place, so I was happy to comply.

Mark sat on a chair by the window and I sat on my bed. I closed my eyes and clasped my hands together as I had seen other people do during my childhood. Mark told me to follow what he was going to pray. I sat with my eyes tightly closed as he began. I didn't understand the significance of his words, but was nevertheless willing to go along with them because I wanted something to happen. It was perhaps from Bible stories I had heard at Sunday school, where people had seen angels and blinding lights, that this expectation had its origins.

Not wanting Mark to notice that I was looking around, I opened my right eye very slightly and peeped through my eyelashes, scanning the little room left and right for any supernatural sign. I really expected something to happen – but nothing did. I didn't hear or see anything out of the ordinary. Mark's words came to a halt and I opened both my eyes. Hiding my disappointment that nothing had happened, I gave him a watery smile. I didn't feel any different. It seemed nothing had happened; neither had I understood what Mark had been saying.

However, he seemed satisfied that I must now be a Christian and, in time, still wondering whether I was doing the right thing, I agreed to be his girlfriend.

Although I had been attracted to this university partly because of the word 'saint' in its name, I had not realised at the time of my application that St Andrews was the ecclesiastical capital of Scotland. Churchgoing was for many students an intrinsic part of their university experience and, once in this new environment, my adolescent scorn of church evaporated. I was eager not to miss out on anything that the university had to offer and decided to add churchgoing to my weekly activities. I didn't know anything about Christian denominationalism so my choice of church was based purely on the location and aesthetic appearance of the building. I decided to attend All Saints, an attractive-looking Scottish episcopal church not far from the ancient cathedral ruins and castle, and a one-minute walk from the North Sea.

I was searching for something meaningful, something significant, perhaps something I had never known before. I could conceive of no other way forward than continuing with my Philosophy studies and getting involved in the life of a church. So I attended the morning service most Sundays, then joined the many other students who were doing the traditional post-church walk along St Andrews pier, all wearing the distinctive St Andrews' scarlet academic gown, reserved for Sundays and special occasions.

Mark joined me in attendance at All Saints, in spite of the fact his church background was very different. His father was an elder in a local evangelical church near where they lived, and his whole family were, to my mind, 'religious'. I hadn't realised at the time that Mark was in what he described as a 'mind-rebellion' against his evangelical church background. This being the case, he was happy to try out a different expression of Christianity. The word 'evangelical' didn't mean anything to me at the time, and I didn't bother enquiring as to its significance.

I started doing voluntary work in the All Saints' bookstore and coffee shop, and joined the choir. As a choir member I wore robes: a white cassock overlaid by a black surplice. I learned the ritualistic routine of turns, genuflections and sung responses which we were expected to perform at set times during the service.

I believed that being religious meant I had to appear very sombre, so as I paraded into the church, following the cross-led procession, I wore a solemn expression and maintained this throughout the service – all designed to impress the congregants, who I believed would consider me truly religious, even saintly. I thought that was what it was all about. During the sermon, however, I would lean my head against the hard wooden back of the choir stalls and daydream. My eyes would come to rest on the stained-glass windows positioned high up in the stone walls. I could hear the rector's voice droning in lofty but dreary tones in the background, and I gleaned little from his message other than that I had a duty to be good to my neighbour.

I wanted to formalise my new-found religiosity and applied to be confirmed. I attended confirmation classes with the rector in the church vestry. Here I learned about the exodus of the Israelites from Egypt and other Old Testament stories. During these sessions I didn't grasp that they might have a personal application to my life, and I have no recollection of learning anything about the New Testament. If the rector covered it, I didn't take it in.

When it came to the confirmation ceremony, I, along with two others, approached the altar with a white scarf tied round my head. With Mark looking on from the pews,

I knelt down. After having various words pronounced over me, I was expected to respond with, 'Peace be with you also.' I was so nervous and lacking in confidence that I couldn't get the words out and had to be prompted by the rector.

Although I lacked certainty about God and Christianity, I felt I was making progress in my quest to be religious and that I was on a more meaningful path than had been the case when I lived at Eastfield. Outwardly I was doing everything in my power to leave my past behind and attain a deeper life of religiosity. Although inwardly I didn't feel any different, I just accepted that as the norm, and have no recollection of anyone telling me otherwise.

One evening I was attending a special event at the church, a Eucharist service preceded by snacks and copious amounts of wine in one of the anterooms. After eating I took a seat next to the aisle and began following the service. Some way through the proceedings there was a loud thud from one of the rear pews. I turned and saw one of the male congregants – a short, plump, bespectacled student, whom I recognised to be someone closely involved with the church – had crashed onto the ornate stone floor, apparently in a drunken stupor. As someone rushed to help him, I turned back to face the front while the service continued, uninterrupted. I felt unsettled. I had thought being religious meant not drinking to excess. I hadn't expected to witness drunkenness in a church. It shook me, and subconsciously I wondered whether I had understood my new religion correctly.

In my second year I chose as my third subject Russian Literature over Philosophy. I had become frustrated by the endless questions Philosophy posed while providing no concrete answers – and it was answers that I needed. I moved to a mixed hall of residence, John Burnet Hall, and was given a room in a nearby newly constructed, prefabricated annex nicknamed the 'shoebox'. I still attended All Saints regularly, as did my boyfriend Mark. At this time I became aware that there was a group of students living below me who had been nicknamed the 'God Squad'. 'Just another quirky student interest,' I thought, as I carried on with my very busy life, which, in addition to my studies and church involvement, included lots of sport, horse riding and spending time with Mark. In addition to teaching me how to drive in the red Beetle, he would take me on regular trips to explore the wilds of Fife and beyond. I had even resumed playing a stringed instrument, having bought a lovely old violin in Leeds, which had been recommended by Mark's mother.

One evening, as I was studying in my room, there came a knock at the door. Thinking it might be Mark, I opened it, but instead of seeing him I saw a diminutive, middle-aged woman wearing a headscarf. She looked me straight in the eye and, without any introduction, asked, 'Are you saved?'

I was taken aback by the strangeness and directness of her question, and wondered how to respond. 'Err, I think so,' I heard myself say.

'You should *know*,' came her pointed reply.

I was in a complete haze. What *did* she mean? I decided the quickest way to get her to leave was by telling her what she wanted to hear.

'Yeah, I am,' I replied, somewhat facetiously, at which point, without enquiring further, she turned away and went to the next room along.

I closed the door and returned to my desk, telling myself she was just a strange woman with some very odd ideas.

Chapter 14
Nearing home

In 1985 Mum came to St Andrews to pay me a visit. My life was happy and busy and I was revelling in the opportunities that university offered. But Mum looked pale and drawn. Andrew had been sentenced to six months in Armley prison in Leeds for smashing several windows at the local shops, some flat windows and a window at the local surgery. At age 23 his behaviour had worsened, and there was a total lack of effective support for him from either social services or medical professionals. I interpreted the window smashing as a cry for help when I heard that Andrew had passively waited until the police arrived.

I will never understand why a medically diagnosed schizophrenic, clearly in a distressed mental state, would be sent to prison. It was unjust – not to say unprofessional. Later, as I thought it over, I wished I had had the confidence and courage to act to help him. But I felt helpless. In addition, I was more than fully occupied digging myself out of the hole I felt I had been in for almost my entire life, and the thought of helping someone else scarcely entered my head at that moment.

The previous year Gramps had died, at the age of 89. Through his eighties he had been fit and active, continuing to swim in the salt-water outdoor pool in Scarborough's South Bay and riding his grey moped. Physically, he had deteriorated rapidly while I was staying at Mum's during the university holidays. I went to visit him regularly as he lay in bed. Mum, Span and I were standing next to the bed one day as he cried out, seemingly oblivious to the fact that we were there, repeatedly saying, 'I'm sorry, I'm sorry, I'm sorry.' I felt a little afraid, for I had no idea what he was sorry about, nor to whom these words were addressed.

Span did her best to take care of him in his last days, but in spite of the scent of the freshly laundered sheets and towels, I could detect another aroma intermingled with the freshness: scarily for me, it was the odour of death. We all knew his end was approaching, and as the days dragged on Gramps was transferred to hospital. It was with some relief, then, that a drawn and ashen-faced Uncle David said to me on Span's doorstep, 'Dad's dead.'

Though I was relieved that the waiting was now over, death to me was an inexplicable and terrible event. Gramps and I had not been especially close, but we had managed to get on well enough. Now I felt shaken by this irreversible and permanent loss. Attending his funeral brought me face to face with the reality of death, but I had no answers, no clear hope of anything beyond this life from which to draw comfort. I simply had to keep going with my young life – without answers.

His death was a significant turning point in our lives. Mum, having inherited quite a significant sum, began to make plans to leave Eastfield and buy her own home. I wanted her to move away from Scarborough, away from all the negative associations of the past ten years. So the historical city of York, where we had enjoyed family day trips, seemed the obvious choice.

I knew Mum, being indecisive, would find it hard to make a firm decision to buy a house, so during the next university break I accompanied her on a trip to York to look for a suitable property. We entered an estate agent's in the city centre and, within minutes, spotted a modern bungalow for sale in the right price range for Mum to buy practically outright.

'That's the one,' I announced, stabbing my finger on the photo of a modern bungalow a few miles from York's centre. It was positioned at the end of a cul-de-sac and backed on to some woods. It reminded me of the pleasant-looking private housing I had often longed to live in as I cycled past on my way to Span's house. I felt so strongly about never again spending time at Eastfield that I threatened to stay away during the holidays unless Mum moved to York. Remarkably and quickly, Mum's purchase was agreed, and consequently my next home visit was in York.

Mark helped Mum to move all our belongings and settle in to her new home. Since I was regularly attending church in St Andrews I wanted to continue the practice during the holidays, so Mark's parents gave me the details of York Evangelical Church, which they thought Mum and I might want to try.

On Sunday we set off on the bus to find it. It was located among some lovely old university buildings known as the King's Manor in the centre of York, close to the art gallery. In the courtyard there was a large sign directing visitors up

145

some old stone stairs. It read, 'York Evangelical Church – All Welcome'.

We were warmly greeted at the door and, as I stepped over the threshold, a number of people came up to me wanting to shake my hand and say hello. One after another they came. I had never before received such an enthusiastic and friendly welcome from total strangers and, although rather surprised, joined in with the enthusiastic hand-shaking and introductions.

Once seated, I had the opportunity to look around, and saw around 40 people on rows of chairs. This was utterly unlike anything I had become used to at the much more formal church in Scotland. Where was the altar? Where were the statues, the ornate stonework, carvings and stained-glass windows? Where were the Stations of the Cross, the high cross and incense? Where were the bells, the order of service, the choir?

I was wondering what was going to happen when a man, wearing a suit and tie, briskly stepped in front of everyone and opened the service. 'Why isn't he wearing a dog collar or a priest's garments?' I wondered. I wasn't used to this and found it all very odd.

After singing one or two hymns and listening to a long talk by the suited man who, it emerged, was the church leader, the meeting ended and people began to mill around talking to their friends and visitors. I was approached by several, one of whom introduced himself as Len. He informed me that he used to belong to the Hell's Angels, a tough motorcycle gang. Encouraged by the interest he showed in me, I began telling him about my church in St Andrews, explaining how different it was from what I had just experienced. To me, the episcopal church was a proper place of worship, whereas this wasn't. I was determined to establish this distinction. Feeling very proud of what I saw as my superior religiosity, I began describing the order of service and the ritual at my church, thinking he would be impressed.

Rather abruptly, and to my great surprise, he jabbed his finger at me, just inches from my face, and said, 'You don't want all that! You want to be saved!'

I was completely taken aback by his apparent dismissal of my religious practice and looked at him, momentarily speechless. 'Err, yeah,' I replied, bemused and feeling somewhat deflated.

Len had expressed his conviction very passionately, but I hadn't the faintest idea what he was talking about. This didn't matter, though, because the welcome I had received from these people was more than enough to encourage me to go back, which I did whenever I was in York.

It was during these visits that I got to know a group of young people my own age, most of whom were also students at different universities across the country, and like me, spent some of their holidays in York.

In the 1986 summer break I began spending more and more time with the visiting students and resident families who attended York Evangelical Church. Not one Sunday would go by when I didn't receive an invitation to someone's home, often from Fran and Terry Hammond, whose practice was to invite students to their home. Sunday became an enjoyable routine: a slap-up two-course meal, chatting and enjoying one another's company and occasionally going for an afternoon walk, before returning

147

to the Hammonds' house for tea. Tea in our part of Yorkshire was the term used for a light evening meal, consisting of an array of sandwiches and light snacks, including sausage rolls, pizza and other tasty savoury morsels alongside cakes, trifle and endless cups of tea, after which we would all then return to church for the evening service. I thoroughly enjoyed this generous hospitality, and even put on a little weight as a result.

Sport, reading newspapers and listening to the radio were discouraged on a Sunday. This was the 'Lord's Day', I was told, and anything which distracted us from keeping it as such was to be avoided. None of this was a problem for me. I enjoyed the fact that there were clear boundaries and I knew where I stood. These people seemed to be very sure about what they believed, and I found that very appealing. I was too busy lapping up their kindness and generosity to concern myself about what should and shouldn't be done on a Sunday. I just couldn't get enough of the love they were showing me.

And yet I knew I wasn't quite like them. I didn't have the same eagerness and conviction when it came to anything Christian. Although I had come to see myself as religious, I still felt I lacked something, but I couldn't put my finger on it.

One Sunday I was listening to the talk but, as at the Christian Union meeting three years earlier, the words were largely meaningless. A fog clouded my mind whenever I heard the Bible being explained. Nevertheless, on this particular occasion I was jolted awake as the speaker made reference to being in heaven. Raising his voice he declared, 'And oh, that we would *all* be there!' and looked straight at me. I was seated towards the back and wondered why he was looking at me. Was he trying to tell me something? Was he suggesting I might not be in heaven? Why *wouldn't* I be? After all, I went to church. I looked and sounded religious, or so I thought. By now I had stopped using the 'f' word and had generally cleaned up my act. There was surely nothing wrong with me, I reasoned… and yet, I couldn't say with absolute certainty whether I would be in heaven or not. I just couldn't fathom the answer to my own question. It was all very unsettling.

Mark and I often went on activity holidays, walking or cycling. The summer of 1986 was no exception and we embarked on a walking holiday along the North Devon coast. Then the strangest thing happened. Out of the blue, I experienced an overwhelming, almost paralysing feeling. I felt as though a very heavy black cloud was hanging over me and I became very subdued. I was normally a bubbly person, full of enthusiasm for life, so Mark noticed straightaway and wondered what on earth the matter was. The distressing feeling persisted and was accompanied by an irresistible longing to return to York. I felt as though a giant magnet were pulling me back there and I had little power or will to resist. I lost all interest in the holiday and told Mark I had to return to York right away. That was all I knew. There was urgency now, so without delay and with a very bemused Mark accompanying me, we returned to Bath, where I caught the first available train back to York. On arrival I was convinced I had done the right thing, but I didn't know why.

I had scarcely been back a day when I received an invitation to Fran's house. She had also invited Don, a fellow member of the young people's group. She recalled the day some years later: 'You were asking us about the claims Christ made about Himself, and looked as though you were about to burst into tears.' I had no personal recollection of this, but learned later from Don that it had caused him to look questioningly at Fran. 'Is Mandy perhaps not a Christian after all?' he had wondered. Given the changes that had taken place in my life during my three years at St Andrews I could have passed myself off as a Christian to people who didn't know me well. Indeed, as far as I was concerned I *was* a Christian, so why all the questions and uncertainty?

Mark, concerned following my sudden departure from our holiday, visited me in York. We took a walk to a small lake not far from Mum's house. I was still experiencing the disturbing feeling which had come over me in Devon and, as we sat down by the water, I suddenly burst into tears. I had always made a point of never crying in front of anyone and could not explain what was happening. All I knew was that I felt deeply unsettled.

Chapter 15
Coming home to Dad

That week was the end of the summer holidays and we students were preparing to return for the new academic year – my fourth and final year at St Andrews. We had a few days left before leaving York.

To wrap up the holiday, several of the group decided to go out for a meal. I was seated at the table at a right angle to Steve. In the short time I had known him I had become struck by the way he stood out from the rest in terms of his Christian commitment. I had the impression he was a particularly keen Christian. He was happy to go the extra mile, and his faith, as I saw it, was the focal point of his life. I had learned that he spent some of his holidays helping out at Christian camps and, although I now considered myself a Christian, I couldn't fathom why *anyone* would want to waste precious holiday time doing *that*. It was a mystery and my curiosity was aroused. There was an indescribable quality to Steve which had caught my attention, but I was unable to pin it down. Deep down I knew I didn't have his enthusiasm and commitment to Christ. Indeed, he wasn't the only one who inadvertently made me realise I lacked something – the zeal of the entire

York church congregation was also causing me to doubt my claim to being a Christian.

Towards the end of the meal, Steve pulled a booklet out of his pocket and pushed it over the table towards me. As I was busy chatting with the person on my left, I thanked him and slipped it into my jacket pocket without comment.

After our farewells I returned home and prepared to go to bed. I emptied my jacket pockets and pulled out the booklet. Glancing at the cover but taking little notice, I tossed it onto the floor next to my bed. 'I'll look at that in the morning,' I told myself. Then I fell asleep.

The next day I awoke at around 10am – it had been a late night. It was 13 September 1986. The bungalow was quiet so I assumed Mum had gone on her usual visit to the shops for the day's groceries.

As I lay on my stomach in bed I suddenly felt overcome by the same inexplicable, low feeling I had had on the walking holiday in North Devon. It was so unlike me. I couldn't understand what was causing it. On the face of it I had everything to look forward to. I lifted my face off the pillow and my eyes came to rest on the small booklet. I reached down to pick it up and placed it on my pillow, and for the first time I looked at it properly. The title of the booklet, as I recall it, was *How to be Filled with the Spirit*, written by Bill Bright and published by Campus Crusade for Christ. On the front cover was the happy face of a young man, about my age. To me religion was a serious matter, so why did he appear so happy?

The booklet was saying that many Christians go through life without ever experiencing the fulfilling and fruitful life which Christ promised to all who trust in Him.

This got my attention. In terms of my Christian connections, I had increasingly felt I was on the outside looking in. As I continued to turn the pages it was as though the booklet were speaking directly to me. The feeling that I was on the periphery couldn't have been because the York church congregation was unfriendly or cliquey. On the contrary, I had never received such an enthusiastic welcome in all my life, and I found the church to be very inclusive. The feeling of incompleteness, my sense that something was wrong, was being caused by something else, but I didn't know what.

As I read on, now taking in every word, I suddenly felt as though a light were gradually illuminating my mind, in the same way a bulb gradually lights up when a dimmer switch is slowly turned. By the time I had reached the middle of the booklet I was totally gripped, and I eagerly read the remaining pages, absorbing every word.

On the very last page there was a prayer which referred to the crucifixion and death of Christ, Who had paid the price for all the wrong things I had done – yes, *I* had done – followed by an invitation for *me* to receive His forgiveness and commit *my* life to following Him. Transfixed, I gawped at the words and gasped. 'What?' I had heard these words before, but now, for the first time, they were intensely personal. I knew I had not made any such commitment – ever.

'Why hasn't anyone told me this is what I need to do?' I said to myself, my thoughts now beginning to tumble over one another in growing excitement. In fact, as I was to later reflect, I had been exposed to calls from a number of people to do exactly this, but had been deaf to them all.

Then – I knew. Suddenly, I *knew*. This was what I had been looking for. Everything in me screamed YES! – the way a person might if they had suddenly found the most incredible, unthinkable treasure after a long, hard search. But now there was nothing more for me to do. Within a split second, everything had changed. I found myself kneeling face down on the green carpet, sobbing and sobbing with gut-wrenching sounds, my arms crossed over my abdomen, crying like I had never cried before. Suddenly I could see – I could see what I had been like: the terrible way I had treated Mum, my wild teenage years, my selfishness, the fact that until now I had shut God out of my life.

The crying went on and on. But these were tears of relief, of joy! I knew I was now forgiven. The relief was immense. I felt as though a heavy weight had been lifted off my shoulders and hurled away. I felt that for the first time in my life I could see. I could SEE! God was at last real to me. I could feel His presence right there in my little bedroom in York. God was real! Everlasting life was a reality I could no longer deny.

The revelations kept coming thick and fast. I realised that I had not been on the path to eternal life until this revolutionary moment. I could only assume I had been heading to a lost eternity, one which Jesus Christ frequently, clearly and unreservedly warned about: Hell. But now, in an instant, in less than a split second, my whole direction in life, in time and eternity, had been changed. All the confusion of the last five years when I had been searching for answers vanished, and I could see clearly now. It seemed as though a thousand pieces of a jigsaw puzzle had miraculously slotted into place. Finally, everything was making sense as the crying went on and on – emptying me of all my guilt.

Eventually, my face wet with tears, I sat back on my haunches on the floor and looked up out of my bedroom window. It was a bright, sunny day and my eyes came to rest on the row of tall conifers which separated Mum's back garden from the woods behind. Then I looked up at the clear blue sky. I had never felt this way before. I experienced a feeling of being totally new, as though I had been recreated. The view from my window looked so different. The colours were more vivid and real than I had ever seen in my life. I felt truly alive and at one with God, my heavenly Father. For the first time in my life I experienced an inexplicable peace and joy. The words 'Jesus died for you', which had echoed in my mind from early childhood, now, incredibly, made sense. Finally I understood that Jesus' death had paid the price for my wrongdoing, and I was set free.

My joy knew no bounds! I stood up, burst out of my bedroom, shot into the lounge and began jumping around, stamping my feet, punching my fists in the air and shouting, 'I've become a Christian! I've become a Christian!'

Mum, who just moments earlier had returned from the shops, was standing in the lounge doorway, holding a carrier bag full of groceries. She looked at me, confused. 'What do you mean?' she asked.

'I've become a Christian!' I kept shouting, continuing to jump around. 'I've become a Christian!'

Within minutes I was on the phone to Mark who, like Mum, had to listen to my exuberant shouting: 'I've become a Christian! It happened just now!'

'But I thought you knew all that,' replied Mark in a small voice. He had been under the impression that I had become a Christian three years earlier.

'NO! NO!' I continued, unable to contain my excitement. 'It's just happened now!' I kept repeating, so swept away by what I had experienced that I didn't give one thought to how Mark might be feeling.

There are insufficient words to fully describe the joy and excitement I experienced at this time. It was beyond anything I could ever have dreamt of or imagined. Insignificant as I believed myself to be, I had now, through Jesus, and against all expectations, entered into relationship with the God of the universe! Little me! I was staggered to think that God would be even remotely interested in me, considering what I had been like. It seemed too good to be true, and yet I knew it *was* true. I just knew that I knew that I knew.

In an instant my whole outlook on life had radically changed. I wanted to tell the whole world what had happened to me. I wanted to climb onto the highest building in York and scream through a megaphone, 'Jesus saves!' I wanted to cross oceans and travel the world, telling everyone everywhere I went what had happened to me and to announce that the same could happen to them. All they had to do was say 'yes' in recognition of their need for Jesus' forgiveness and they too would experience new birth and new life. What was there to compare with *this*?

Riding my bike to church a few days later while listening through headphones to a Christian message by the world-renowned evangelist, Billy Graham, I had more energy than I had ever known. I wanted to rush up to people and stick the headphones on their ears and shout, 'Listen to *this*!' I had been severely tempted to do so when I saw a student sitting and reading quietly outside York town library but, thankfully, remembering my own previous confusion, I decided against it.

This was *it*. Now I knew why I had felt as a child that something special was going to happen to me. At long last I had been shown the wonderful thing that I had felt destined for: that special thing, which wasn't a thing at all, but a person – Jesus Christ.

The words 'Jesus died for you', which had been mere words echoing in my mind until now, were suddenly the most important words in the world, and I was amazed by my own previous inability to understand them.

The questions I had carried around for so long were now gloriously answered, including the niggling one about the purpose of Sunday. It was all so clear now. The fog had cleared, the mist dissolved. Gone were the days of being religious, of trying to be a Christian by leading an apparently 'good' life. I realised it had nothing whatsoever to do with my attempts to be good. It was purely to do with what Jesus had achieved on the cross – nothing more, nothing less.

Now I understood what the strange woman at my door in St Andrews had meant when she had asked me, 'Are you saved?' Now I could see what Len had been so enthusiastic about when he poked his finger in my face, telling me that it wasn't religion I needed but salvation. I finally grasped why the people at church were so excited about their faith, and I understood the reason Steve had spent his holidays at Christian youth camps. I had been so blind and deaf and hadn't even known it.

The news of my conversion soon reached the ears of the people at church. Now I truly belonged. 'I hear we can call you "sister" now,' said one person, as I stood grinning from ear to ear.

'Congratulations on becoming a Christian,' said Steve's brother, turning round in his seat as I sat waiting for the church meeting to begin.

'I didn't do anything,' I replied, still feeling shell-shocked by the momentous turnaround in my life. And I truly hadn't done anything. It had all been done for me. All I'd had to say was 'yes' to Jesus. I recognised that I had been on a search for Him, but in the end it was through an encounter, through a revelation that God the Father had made Himself known to me. I had been lost and He had come to find me. The glorious thing was that I didn't need anyone to tell me what had happened. I *knew*.

I was eager to start reading the Bible. I was hungry for it and began reading the Gospel of John, absorbing the words, taking them right into the core of my being, like rich, nourishing food.

I wrote to Steve, who had already left York to start his new term in Newcastle. I received a five-page letter almost by return of post enthusing about what had happened and expressing his total joy and surprise at this unexpected turn of events. It turned out that he had not even realised I wasn't a Christian and had given me the booklet thinking that perhaps I needed to understand more about the Holy Spirit. He was as surprised by events as I was, but was filled with joy and told me he had been praying for the whole year that Jesus would be seen in him. He said his prayer had been answered in a way which went way beyond his expectations.

I wrote a very long letter to Joanna telling her what had happened to me. She later confided in me that she had read the letter while sitting on the toilet and had burst into tears. To her, this signalled the possible end of our friendship, perhaps because she thought I had been brainwashed by a strange cult. But to me it was the beginning of much deeper and wonderful relationships, not just with my new-found worldwide Christian family, but with everyone who knew me.

When my uncle came to hear of it on his next visit to Mum's house, he stood in the lounge looking at me with an expression of troubled uncertainty. 'I wouldn't take it too seriously if I were you, Mandy,' he said, concerned that I had been unhealthily influenced by some people with strange ideas. 'If you're still saying the same thing two years from now, I might begin to think there's something in it,' he added. No amount of enthusiasm and reassurances on my side sufficed to convince him, and from this point my views on the existence of God, of life and of death, would sharply differ from his own. My down-to-earth uncle, who had always been my role model, now appeared to stand in stark opposition to what was most important to me – my new-found treasure – Jesus Christ. Although we were still in a friendly uncle–niece relationship, we were no longer on the same page or in easy agreement about spiritual things. Jesus Christ had swept me into His life and turned mine upside down. Nothing would ever be the same again. *I* would never be the same again.

I returned to York to get baptised as a believer four months after I had become a follower of Jesus. I gave a short account to the gathered church about how I had become a Christian. 'You can fool people but you can't fool God,' I added at the end. My story showed that no matter what we or others might think of where we stand in matters of faith, God is the only one who knows the true attitude of our hearts towards Him. Mum commented to someone at the baptism that after her initial confusion about my coming to faith, she had later experienced a sense of relief because, 'Finally,' as she put it, 'someone has got Mandy under control.'

We then went to the swimming pool where the baptism was to take place. I put on my swimming costume and a white gown. I stepped into the water and waded over to the church leader and one of the elders. After being asked if I had received Jesus as my Lord and Saviour I was plunged fully into the water. The baptism was symbolic that the old me had died and I was now a new person, recreated in Christ Jesus.

As I came up to the surface the gathered church burst into song, and I was enveloped by a complete joy and peace which fell on me like a blanket. Grinning broadly, I felt caught up in God's presence, and this feeling remained with me all the way back to St Andrews. Sitting on the train to Edinburgh, watching the northern landscape flash past, I felt as though I were floating on a cloud, independent of my surroundings. I was filled with an unceasing and indescribable joy.

I was most anxious to tell Dad about my new-found faith. It was nearly two years since I had received a letter from him – the only one since his declaration that I was no longer his daughter. In it he had told me he couldn't believe he was about to turn 50. Throughout this time he had not disclosed his address so I had to post all my letters to the Scarborough court, where they would be forwarded.

I picked up my pen and wrote, 'Dear Dad, I hope you are well…' This was how Andrew and I always began our letters to him. It was like a formula we followed when communicating with him rather than being spontaneous. This stiffness and tongue-tied manner of speaking and writing had always been a mark of my communication with Dad throughout my teenage years. But now I was writing to him about something that meant everything to me, something so radical and life-changing I thought he couldn't fail to catch my enthusiasm and would reply immediately.

Becoming a Christian had revolutionised the way I viewed people, and this included Dad and Ella. I had come face to face with the fact that I myself had done wrong and that I needed God's forgiveness. This automatically resulted in a realisation that other people, including Dad and Ella, were also in need of forgiveness, and that Jesus had died for them too. I tried to explain these things in my letter to Dad, adding that for me the past was now irrelevant and I was ready to make a fresh start. I made it clear I held no grudges and had forgiven everyone, including myself, for everything that had happened. At the time I was so overwhelmed by the realisation that *I* had been forgiven that there was no room for unforgiveness or resentment.

I posted my letter from St Andrews and waited expectantly for what I was sure would be a card or letter from Dad agreeing to my idea of a fresh start and, hopefully, a reconciliation.

But nothing came.

Chapter 16
The healing begins

I returned to St Andrews no longer the same person who had left at the end of my third year. I was what the biblical Paul called a 'new creation' (2 Corinthians 5:17). Walking down the street I bumped into a member of the 'God Squad' and relayed to her what had happened to me; it was met with lots of joyful laughter and hugs. It emerged that the 'God Squad' had been praying for all the students in the university's residential 'shoebox' where I had been living. Their praying for me was one of many things I would look back on as signs of God's intervention in my life long before I came to know Him personally.

From the very outset of my new life as a Christian, I viewed God as Father. I had been privileged to receive deep and rich Bible teaching while at the York church, including the doctrine of the Trinity: God the Father, God the Son (Jesus) and God the Holy Spirit as co-equals in the Godhead, but with distinct roles. Yet, whenever I prayed it was invariably to God the Father, and I didn't trouble myself as to the mystery of how Jesus and the Holy Spirit functioned in harmony within that.

As a Daughter of the King I was now in a position to receive the healing I needed, although at the time I didn't think I was in need of any such thing. The thought of restoration and wholeness never occurred to me. I believed I was just fine now: wrongs forgiven, at peace with God my creator, prayers to offer and to expect a response... But gradually, over time, I began to understand that God had begun a lifelong healing work as soon as I had chosen to follow Jesus.

From my earliest days as a genuine Christian, people began coming across my path who were significant in the healing process. It had started with the people at York Evangelical Church, who had been the first to embrace me as a stranger and had seen my transition from a place of religious striving to one of new life and relationship with God. They were the first in what became a series of wonderful people over the years who I believe God used to begin to make me whole.

Two such were Siobhan and Ralph, whom I met when I began to attend St Andrews Baptist Church after I returned to St Andrews as a new Christian. They were an interesting retired couple: professional, educated, well travelled. It was through Siobhan that I was able to build on the strong foundations laid for me at York Evangelical Church. She ran a course in foundational biblical truths for new believers, which I eagerly attended. I wanted to soak up all the 'living water' of Jesus that I could get (John 7:38). This was the knowledge I had been searching for, and I wanted to mature in my understanding of the gospel: the good news of Jesus.

Having committed my life to God, my day-to-day confidence greatly increased. My feelings of unworthiness were slowly being replaced by the certainty that in spite of my past behaviour, I was of great value to God. I knew I was loved, forgiven and accepted. I had entered into a relationship with my creator, my heavenly Father, and regardless of whether anyone else believed it, I was now a citizen of His kingdom and a member of the worldwide family of God.

After graduating I wanted to go immediately into full-time Christian service. Mark had started to talk about getting engaged, yet I sensed my relationship with him beginning to teeter. My decision to follow Jesus had led to an almost immediate desire to undertake Christian service abroad, but Mark didn't appear to be motivated in this way. He seemed content to remain in the UK.

I spent my first summer after graduating with a Christian organisation called Operation Mobilisation. With them I travelled to Vienna and joined a team taking the good news about Jesus to tourists there. My experience in Vienna was so exciting that I wanted to continue with the organisation by joining one of their ships: the *Logos* or the *Doulos*. The ships sailed around the world taking Bibles and Christian literature to people. I was ready to pack my bags and go. However, once back in York after graduating, my church leader discouraged this, believing I needed to gain some experience in the ordinary world of work and become more established in my faith before venturing into more challenging situations. As a result, in 1988, a few months after graduating, I moved down to London to study for a CertTEFLA, a teacher training programme which would qualify me to teach English to foreign students.

It was during my first few months in London that Mark and I finally decided that our lives were indeed going in different directions, and the wisest thing to do was to put an end to our relationship. 'You'll be glad one day,' I told him.

Yet there was a sadness to the parting. Having known each other for more than five years, we had shared many things together, and the relationship had been good for me. Before I had committed my life to Jesus I had not been interested in marriage, but that had started to change. So it was ironic that my relationship with Mark ended. Yet I believed I would eventually meet Mr Right, someone who shared my desire to take the good news of Jesus to people overseas. That was my expectation as I went through my twenties.

I landed my first job at an international school of English in Greenwich. Here I taught English to adult foreign students from around the world. During the two years I worked there, I thoroughly enjoyed the opportunities to get to know the students and learn more about their countries and cultures. I made the acquaintance of many students from the Middle East and North Africa, and this often led to lively discussions about the Christian faith and how it compared with world religions.

I wanted to spend my life telling people about Jesus, and that desire, strengthened by my interest in other cultures and travel, led me to apply to All Nations Christian College in Hertfordshire, a college which trained people for Christian ministry and missions at home and abroad. My intention was to enter Christian service in the Middle East. It was spring 1990.

At the time I was attending the People's Hall, otherwise known as 'The Slade', in Plumstead, south-east London. Having recognised my desire to spread the good news of Jesus, they offered to pay all my study fees and accommodation expenses, but asked me to live by faith for any additional costs. What a wonderful, God-given opportunity now stood before me! All Nations was my first choice of training college, and I had set my heart on going there in September of that year.

I attended an interview and was asked to step outside while two staff members discussed my application. I was very sure I was in the right place and it would all work out. The door opened and I was invited back into the room. 'We'd like to offer you a place,' they began, 'but not for this year – for next.'

What?! I was shocked. I had been so sure that this was the right next move for me. I couldn't believe it, and this must have shown on my face as I turned away and left. Walking away down the winding country lane which led to the college, I felt shattered. I couldn't easily accept that this had happened.

Crestfallen, I returned home and rang one of my church leaders to report the news. As far as I was concerned, the only appealing option was now a closed one – at least for a year.

Over the next few weeks I discussed various alternatives with my church leaders, the main one being to spend the year with a missionary organisation in Djibouti. Djibouti? In the horn of Africa? This wasn't what I had in mind at all. My interest lay in the Middle East.

Over the coming months I battled with the prospect of going to a country I didn't feel drawn to. Could I trust my heavenly Father with my life such that I was willing to go anywhere and do anything? This was the challenge I faced throughout the summer of 1990. To clarify my thoughts I took an exploratory trip to Jordan and Egypt to get a clearer idea of what Christian service in the Middle East might be like.

I had been a Christian less than four years, and up until this point things had worked out remarkably smoothly for me. But now I was faced with a situation where things had not gone as I had hoped and planned. I began to waiver, entertaining thoughts that perhaps the God I had committed to intended to lead me down an unbearably hard path. Doubts began to assail me. What if I ended up lonely and miserable, regretting my decision to serve Him?

On my return from the Middle East in August, a pile of letters was waiting for me. It was approaching the end of summer and still no decision had been made about my future. I began opening the letters one by one. Then I came to a slim, white envelope with a Hertfordshire postmark on it. I held the envelope, staring at it, thoughts about what it might contain racing through my mind. I tore open the seal and immediately saw the All Nations logo. Several students had not been able to take up their places at the college that year and would I be interested in beginning my study programme this September? *Would I be interested?* That was an understatement!

I shot to the phone and rang one of my church leaders. What should I do? Should it be Djibouti or All Nations? I knew what I wanted but would he see it that way? Without hesitating, he agreed I should go to All Nations. At the eleventh hour my heart's desire had been granted. I rejoiced in God's incredible goodness to me.

I considered myself to be thoroughly familiar with biblical truth and doctrine and more or less sorted in most areas of my life. But two years of residential study at All Nations would soon cure me of that! Apart from discovering how little I knew about the Bible and Christian ministry, it soon became clear that there was more to All Nations than I had realised. The college emphasised the need for wholeness as a vital part of students' preparation. This meant addressing past wounds and areas of our lives that had been blighted by trauma, such as unresolved relationships or difficult circumstances. Initially I didn't pay too much attention to any talk about healing and wholeness. It wasn't something I wanted to focus on because, as I had decided long ago as a young girl, I was not going to be a victim. I was fine – or so I believed.

However, the college was not willing to lightly brush aside the need to address these deep matters. As people who were being prepared to serve God in all corners of the earth, we were required to receive holistic training, and for most, if not all, that meant coming face to face with the emotional, psychological and spiritual baggage we might be carrying. Each student was allocated a tutor, and it was during sessions with the tutor that conversations could become very personal.

My tutor in my second year was Elizabeth Goldsmith, who had spent many years in Christian service in the Far East with her husband, Martin. Her own story of separation from her missionary parents in China, followed by mother-loss when she was very young during the Second World War, made her the ideal person to empathise with my story, which I told her in my usual matter-of-fact way. I had by now become so used to the chaos in my family – my brother's ongoing illness and Dad's unwillingness to have anything to do with me, not to mention Mum's emotional struggles which, though significantly improved, could occasionally surface – that I talked about it very casually, much as someone might describe walking to the shops to buy a loaf of bread. It was just the way things were, and it seemed as though I couldn't change them even if I wanted to.

To illustrate, a recent visit to Andrew, now living alone in a bedsit in Scarborough's old town, had seen Mum and me hammering on his door, begging to be let in. We were concerned because he had ignored all our attempts to visit him that day. When he finally allowed us in it appeared he had been lying on his bed, suffering from psychotic thoughts. Ten years after his health had started to deteriorate, there was still no sign of recovery.

Of course, these things did affect me, possibly profoundly, but the vast majority of the time they lay dormant, and would only rise to the surface when something happened which hooked into the scar tissue of emotional and psychological wounding that had taken place in my life. And sitting in Elizabeth's study was one of those times.

As my story unfolded she sat, quietly listening, nodding encouragingly from time to time. Then when I had finished, she sighed and said in her gentle voice, 'It's a catalogue of trauma.' She asked me whether I would like to spend time going over the memories, praying and asking God for healing. Having never wanted to be a victim, I didn't do vulnerability very well, and I felt uncomfortable. I still believed I didn't need to go through any healing; nevertheless, surely it could do no harm, so I agreed go along with whatever she suggested.

Elizabeth asked me to close my eyes and to try to imagine myself as a six-year-old living in Marton, thinking in particular of the times when Andrew and I had stood at his bedroom window looking out at the smog-ridden orange sky, longing to escape. 'Where is God at this time?' Elizabeth asked me.

Of course, if she had asked me that all those years ago I would not have understood her question, but now, as someone who had experienced God and who knew that He was real, I was able to respond, 'He is here – with us in the bedroom.'

'What is His expression?' she continued.

'Sorrowful… compassionate,' I answered.

'What do you think He wants you to know?' she asked.

'That He's here with me and that one day everything's going to be all right.'

The questions and answers continued in this way for some time as Elizabeth helped me to relive the memories from my early childhood, all the time bringing God into the picture.

I believed, since committing my life to following God, that He had been present all the time even though Andrew and I might have felt alone in our situation. Now that I was in relationship with God, the pain of the past seemed to be less intense and I could see things in a new light. It wasn't that God had approved of everything that had happened to Mum, Andrew and me – far from it. But I came to realise that our free will can be exercised for either good or bad purposes. If anyone in my past had chosen to exercise theirs in a selfish way, I knew I had to go on forgiving them. Immediately following the euphoria of committing my life to God, it had been so easy to forgive, but over the four years since then there had been occasions when I realised I needed to do it again.

I could tell that Elizabeth, as my tutor, understood my pain. I glanced down and noticed a ladder in her tights. This didn't appear to bother her and went with her natural, unassuming personality. Here was a woman I could look up to. She did not wear thick make-up or fancy clothes; she didn't paint her nails. I knew I was in the company of someone special: a God-lady who, as a child, had been through much pain and struggle herself yet had put God before anything or anyone in her life, and this helped me to trust her as I shared my story.

I continued, looking back at other memories which required healing. But at a point in the session I unexpectedly felt overwhelmed and, experiencing a physical sensation of pressure over the top of my head, burst into tears. The tears seemed to come right from my gut and were uncontrollable. All my life, from the time when I had sat on my bed scowling at Ella and promising myself I would never let anyone see me cry, I had, barring the uncontrollable sobbing at the lake with Mark, succeeded. But here I was, aged 26, crying like a baby in front of Elizabeth.

It was out of character for me to do this. It was so unlike me to display weakness and helplessness, but it had happened seemingly against my will. It seemed God had taken over my emotions, that being the only way I could let the pain out.

I experienced a similar gut-wrenching feeling when I visited an All Nations lecturer. He lived with his family in a house in the college grounds and I went there with another student. While we were chatting, his young daughter, aged around six years, entered the room. Even though he was in the middle of a conversation with us, he reached down and affectionately placed his arm around her. Watching, I felt a slight choking sensation in my throat and knew if I didn't take complete control I might burst into tears. Was this what I had been missing all those years ago – a father's tender touch? 'So this is how a father is meant to be,' I told myself. I continued to watch as he listened to her. Then he gently replied and, satisfied with his response, she skipped happily away. Watching this scene was one more reminder that I had missed the experience of an earthly father. It was a painful thought.

Elizabeth encouraged me to write a detailed essay, exploring how the trajectory of one's life can be affected by their parents' divorce, and this writing became a way of processing much of what had taken place in my childhood – things which I had assumed were no longer an issue for me. The time I spent doing this proved to be very enlightening, the essay having a cathartic effect – another step on the path to wholeness.

Part of my healing journey included making trips back to Marton, Hornsea and Eastfield to look at the houses,

173

schools and places associated with my childhood. From my new Christian perspective I was now able to bring God into those memories, recognising He had been there all along, drawing me to Himself from the youngest age. I no longer saw council estates like Eastfield as the kind of places to avoid or escape from, but 'good soil' in which the good news of Jesus, the gospel, could be 'planted'.

While at All Nations I tried once again to make contact with Dad. I can't recollect how I obtained his telephone number, but I decided to call him and ask if I may visit him. Ella, whom he had eventually married, answered the phone. It was the first time I had heard her voice in 16 years, but the tone and accent were still familiar. It was a strange feeling listening to Ella speak, remembering the past yet now viewing it from a different perspective. My own outlook on life had changed so much after becoming a follower of Jesus that I naively assumed other people would have moved on too and felt optimistic that I would soon be reconciled to Dad.

After I had introduced myself, Ella called for Dad.

'It's your Mandy on the phone,' she said.

After a few moments of silence I heard Dad take the phone. 'Now then, how are you?' he said, in a clipped, businesslike way. This hadn't been what I had expected to hear, and I felt taken aback. Struggling to find the words, I told him I had been wondering whether I could pay him a visit. Possibly feeling put on the spot, and to my surprise, he agreed. So we set a day and time. I had felt anxious about the call, but now I was hopeful that the reconciliation I had been trying to achieve would finally take place.

We had agreed to meet during the college holiday. I was visiting Span at this time and on the Friday before the visit I rang Dad from her house to check that the arrangement we had made was still convenient. Looking back, I wish I hadn't made the call. I told Ella, now Dad's wife, that I just wanted to confirm my visit, but she immediately responded by telling me he didn't want to see me. I was staggered that I had got this far only for it to backfire. She went on to say that she and Dad had nothing in common with me and that they would live their lives and I should live mine. Nothing in common? 'He's only my dad,' I thought. I told her I would rather hear this from Dad, thinking that perhaps she was hijacking my attempts to see him. Then her tone changed, and in a low, almost threatening voice, she told me I had no idea what I had done to them. I was completely aghast. What on earth did she mean? I reminded her that I had been a young child at the time, but her only response was to repeat that we had nothing in common.

I was nonplussed by her audacity and could feel prickles of anger rising on the back of my neck. Who did she think she was? It was outrageous. Earlier in my life this might have resulted in a whole string of expletives or, if she had been within reach, a hard slap across the face. However, on this occasion, I felt a counter-intuitive restraint. It seemed so hard not to blurt out my anger and frustration. But instead my words came out, strained in tone, telling her that I was clearly wasting my time. I then replaced the handset, and that was the last time I ever had direct contact with her – or Dad.

If it really were the case that he didn't want to see me, then why would I want to turn up at his house to a frosty reception? Was it really worth the risk of being rejected again? I decided to let it lie. The day of visiting came and went. The things that could have happened didn't happen. Why not? Was it because of deception? Had his wife been honest about what Dad really wanted? Had he given his approval to her chasing me away like that? It was beyond my comprehension. I had come so close to seeing Dad again, then at the last minute it had been snatched away. I shouldn't have called to confirm, I chastised myself. If only I hadn't picked up the phone to make that unnecessary call – after all, the visit had been arranged – all I had had to do was turn up. Now my attempts at reconciliation lay in tatters again.

Chapter 17
Struggles and departure

My two years at All Nations led to a totally unexpected change of direction in my life. I no longer believed I was cut out for life in the Middle East. In its place I had developed a passion for southern Africa, in particular South Africa.

However, after leaving All Nations I began to struggle. Things had not worked out as smoothly as I had hoped, and I was unsure of the way forward. I had hoped that by now I would have at least met, if not married, a committed Christian bound for Christian service overseas. However, the ratio of single women to men at All Nations had been such that although quite a number of the female students had met their husbands there, an even greater number had not, and I was one of them. I had dated one of the male students for a while but it had been clear to everyone, and eventually to me and him, that we were completely unsuited. I had waited patiently, and prayed, for the right marriage partner for six years, and there was still no sign of a suitable match.

People, including Mum and Uncle David, who was by now a married father of four, occasionally questioned why I was still single, to which I replied that I was equally mystified by it. Prior to committing my life to Jesus there had been no shortage of young men around to get to know. However, as a follower of Jesus I suddenly found myself in a kind of 'no-man's land' where there appeared to be few single men to choose from, and even fewer preparing to go into overseas Christian service. Women outnumbered men at every church I went to, and Christian missionary conferences were even worse. It seemed my desire to serve Christ overseas would come at a cost. I had seen numbers of my Christian friends get married and had read in Christian books stories of marriages made in heaven where two Christians had seemingly been brought together by God. 'Why can't something like that happen to me?' I reasoned. Yet there appeared to be no answers.

I knew I still wanted to go to southern Africa but was unclear about how that would happen. So, with the support of my church, I spent six months working among the homeless with London City Mission, taking food to people who lived in London's 'Cardboard City', a shanty town situated in the shadow of Waterloo Station. Then in 1993 I moved to Brixton to help with a church which had recently been started. I rented a flat above a second-hand bookshop on Coldharbour Lane, Brixton's frontline.

My struggle with singleness did not go away. I had been taught that it would be unwise to embark on a marriage with someone who didn't share my faith, but should wait patiently for God's leading to marriage or singleness. The prospect of lifelong singleness, followed by inevitable childlessness, made me shudder! Given my own difficult experiences as a child I felt, probably wrongly, that it was only fair I should have the opportunity to start a happy family of my own.

Throughout my twenties I had had more male friends than female, and although I accepted my male friends and enjoyed their friendship very much, I had already identified things about each of them which disqualified them from being potential marriage partners. In some cases it was simply because the man in question wasn't a Christian. In others, he might have been a Christian but had significant hang-ups, or his Christian commitment wasn't as strong as I would have liked. I was, in fact, very critical of men when viewing them from a marriage perspective, and within minutes of meeting someone I would have identified at least one reason why he was not marriage material. I disliked any hint of weakness or lack of drive and ambition. I wanted a life partner who was committed to God, someone with a strong sense of identity and purpose.

No doubt my standards were unrealistically high and my evaluation of these men possibly faulty. I was warned by a male friend to change my assessment, otherwise I would never get married.

I have speculated that it was my experience of Dad which lay behind much of my fussiness when it came to choosing a marriage partner. I had seen how disastrous my parents' marriage had been and the destruction which had followed in its wake. 'Can any man be trusted?' I wondered. I needed to be sure that what had happened to Mum wouldn't happen to me.

I also had my share of men who I was interested in but who weren't interested me, and vice versa. It was all very frustrating. Unfortunately, this impasse concerning marriage caused me to become rather angry with God. I began to rebel, wanting to take back control of my own life. Although still involved with Christian activity, I lost my earlier enthusiasm for telling people about Jesus. I began to simply go through the motions of attending church, and for one year even quit church altogether. I became increasingly unhappy. In spite of this, I never once doubted that the good news of Jesus was true. In the midst of my rebellion, I knew that I missed my heavenly Father and that He was still there patiently waiting for me to come to my senses.

My desire to live in southern Africa had not waned in spite of my spiritual laxness, and Brixton proved to be a fascinating multiracial community where I had opportunities to develop my interest in this. I enrolled on a community education course in African Studies and began volunteering at the Africa Centre in London's Covent Garden. While there, I got to know Thumelo, a young South African man living in London. Seeing I had a keen interest in southern Africa, he invited me to his parents' home in Johannesburg. I readily accepted, excited by the prospect of visiting a country I had read so much about and hoped one day to live in.

I found a cheap fight which took me to South Africa's neighbour, Botswana, where I stayed overnight with a Ghanaian family who, the next day, took me to the border and helped me hitch a lift on a juggernaut bound for Johannesburg. I thoroughly enjoyed the adventure of travelling in this way, and chatted happily with the Zimbabwean trucker. Once I had been dropped off on the outskirts of Johannesburg, I had the rather hair-raising experience of not knowing exactly where I was. I wandered into a downtown community where I appeared to be the only white person in sight. My rucksack and camera gave away the fact I was a tourist and, knowing South Africa's reputation for crime, I feared I might not reach my destination in one piece. I was due to meet Thumelo at Park Station, a large transport terminal in Johannesburg. Thankfully, a young local man led me safely to a taxi rank where I boarded a minibus bound for Park Station.

During my visit I was escorted around Katlehong and Thokoza townships, where I enjoyed overwhelmingly warm hospitality from Thumelo's large extended family and network, which even included a visit to a witch doctor. I was bowled over by the kindness extended to me, and by the end of my ten-day visit I was smitten by the country and its people.

It was after this visit that, desperate to find a way forward, I turned to prayer. I knew I wanted to return to South Africa, but how? Although still in my rebellious phase, I now knew there could be no way forward for me unless I involved God. So I knelt down on the floor in my flat and asked Him what I should do. It had never been my experience to hear an audible voice during prayer, but a clear thought came into my mind: 'Do a PGCE.' It came to me so clearly and simply.

A PGCE was a postgraduate teacher training course which would qualify me to teach in secondary schools. Yet this was something I had never wanted to do, having seen the trials of my teachers at Pindar School. However, it dawned on me that this could be my route to a job in South

181

Africa and, seeing no other viable options, I decided to go ahead, much to the incredulity of friends. 'Are you *sure* you want to do *that*?' they asked, knowing how tough secondary teaching could be.

Remarkably, as I approached the end of the course, I came across a recruitment advert in a national newspaper. The British Council was recruiting teachers on behalf of the Botswana Ministry of Education. Having only passed though Botswana briefly, I knew little about it, but reasoned I could make the transition to South Africa at some future point.

After a successful application I began preparing to leave for Botswana in September 1997. Shortly before I was due to fly out and begin my new job, I travelled to Yorkshire to spend time with Mum and Andrew.

I hired a car and Mum and I set off for Scarborough to visit Andrew. About halfway there Mum started to talk, questioning why I was going so far away. She thought perhaps I had no sense of belonging in the UK, that having grown up without a father, I felt rootless, not seeing my country of birth as my home and believing there was nothing to keep me here. Such thoughts had never occurred to me, but I wondered at the time whether there might be some truth to them. Then, after a brief lull in the conversation, Mum burst into tears.

It made sense. She was living alone, obviously very concerned that her only son, who had been ill for 16 years, was living a marginal existence in the town where he had grown up, and had no obvious prospects. The biggest blow was that in spite of endless medication, Andrew's health failed to improve. He was now living in residential care, alongside other people with mental health issues – an environment I believed was not entirely helpful.

I had listened many times to Andrew as he told me about his thoughts. He was convinced that Jim, his former employer at the holiday camp, was controlling him and that everything in life was 'a blast': insubstantial and lacking reality. He believed he was only about 'one inch high', existing only for 'just a few seconds in a big machine'. He told me that this mortal day-to-day life wasn't real, that he wasn't permitted by Jim to have any feelings, nor did Jim want anyone to know that he was controlling Andrew. He occasionally added, 'Jim told me I've got real life coming to me.'

I often pondered on this, wondering from where, or perhaps from whom, this thought had come. If Jim 'told' him to do something, he did it. Thankfully this never led to anything more serious than Andrew occasionally shaving his eyebrows off or, conversely, growing a beard. No amount of reasoned argument from me made any difference. Try as we might, there was nothing Mum and I could do. In addition, he looked odd. The motorbike accident had left him with a limp and he walked with a stoop, one shoulder drooping and his head bent downwards. All we could do was pray and let him know that we cared and wouldn't abandon him.

As I saw it, Andrew had been examined by doctors, psychiatrists and social workers throughout his illness but, as far as I knew, none had recognised his family background as a cause of his problems. No long-term counselling had been offered – only medication. There was one exception. A carer at his first residential home was very concerned about Andrew and found his situation personally distressing. She told me his was the saddest story she had encountered throughout her career. In her opinion, the characteristics he displayed were those of a traumatised child. At last there was someone who cared and had some insight, yet even she appeared powerless to bring meaningful change to his life.

Throughout his life, Andrew had continued to walk the streets of his home town of Scarborough, streets where he had memories of us as children going to watch *Batman* at the cinema, swimming at the indoor and outdoor pools and riding our bikes to watch the mighty North Sea pounding against the sea wall, sending waves up to 15 metres into the air. Except for Mum's weekly visits and my biannual ones, Andrew now walked these streets alone. I often cried when I thought about him – and still do.

Throughout Andrew's illness Dad hadn't involved himself. Mum informed me that after a court hearing during the early 1990s to do with maintenance, she had told Dad of her concern about Andrew. But Dad's response had been, 'Oh, I don't know anything about that,' after which he had turned on his heel and walked away.

And now I, her only daughter, having spent four years in Scotland before moving south, was about to fly thousands of miles away to take up a job offer in Africa. 'Why does it have to be so far away?' she lamented. It was a valid question. All I knew was that I desperately wanted to fulfil my dream of living in Africa. I firmly believed it was my Christian calling. Mum feared I would lose contact with her altogether. I had no intention of ever letting that happen, but it was nevertheless real to her. As we continued with our journey to Scarborough, it made sense for her to cry; there was a lot to cry about.

Once at the residential care home we didn't hang around. I found the atmosphere there quite oppressive. Over the years, I had visited Andrew many times at the residential homes and had observed the other residents, both short-term and long-term: some were talkative and outgoing while exhibiting peculiar behaviour; others quiet and introverted, 'frozen in time'. I marvelled how Andrew maintained any semblance of sanity staying there.

As it was a special occasion, we headed for a hotel to have a snack and tea. We found one on the South Cliff close by. I saw my impending emigration as a significant moment in my life and was expecting some kind of response from Andrew, but he appeared his usual introverted self. Any questions I put to him were met with monosyllables. Eventually the conversation dried up, so Mum nagged him one more time to stop smoking, something she had been doing for the best part of 20 years.

When it came to saying goodbye, Andrew simply stood up and, without speaking, walked out of the hotel lounge. It was as if I lived round the corner and he would be seeing me again the following day. The fact that I was about to leave for London to board a plane for a destination thousands of miles away on another continent with no idea of when I would return provoked not the least response from him. I craned my neck so I could gaze through the large bay window and watch him limp away down the street. He didn't appear to feel a thing, and I found the parting surreal, like some kind of time warp. My own life was moving on, but Andrew's stood still.

The day of my departure arrived. Joanna and Mum accompanied me to Heathrow. Joanna was bubbly and excited, for adventure and starting a new life were things she relished. Mum, however, looked pale and drawn. It was hard for her to watch me leave, but there was no doubt in my mind. I fully intended to maintain contact with my family and return to the UK for visits. To do anything else would have been unthinkable. I was deeply committed to family, such as it was, notwithstanding I would now be living on a different continent.

I had written to Dad via the law courts, telling him about my plans to work in Botswana. He had not replied. As I embarked on my new life, I had no idea whether he had even given me a second thought.

At the airport, after passport control, I left Mum and Joanna behind and walked away, continually turning and waving until they were out of sight. My dream of living in southern Africa was about to come true.

Chapter 18
Father's love

When I stepped out of the plane onto the steps leading down to the tarmac at Sir Seretse Khama Airport near Botswana's capital city, Gaborone, I gasped as a wall of intense, dry heat hit me. I screwed up my eyes against the unexpected glare of the sun reflecting off the modest airport complex in front of me. Botswana, once a British protectorate, had only been independent since 1966. I just had time to take in the vast, clear blue, cloudless sky before being ushered into the airport arrivals area.

As I exited the airport complex, which wasn't much bigger than a primary school, I walked past some exotic-looking green plants and wondered how much water it took to keep them alive in this heat. Then I boarded the hotel bus to the Grand Palm, where I and some 30 other British teachers would be staying for ten days of induction and language learning before being posted to our respective schools.

I had asked to be as close to the South African border as possible because I had plans to undertake some distance learning with the University of South Africa. After an initial tussle with the Ministry of Education, which wanted to send me to the Central Kalahari, miles from anywhere, I was posted to Diratsame II Community Junior Secondary School in Moshupa, a village situated 65 kilometres from the capital.

Dropped off at last at the small bungalow allocated to me on the school campus, I sat down on the shipping container which had arrived with me and held almost everything I owned. Looking out of the front window at the one-storey classrooms and dry, dusty earth, I wondered what I had let myself in for.

No one came to welcome me or show me any local facilities. I had a small food supply, but was unsure where to go for more. I later came to realise that in Botswana newcomers were expected to present themselves to the people they had come to live among, rather than wait to be invited. I had to learn this the hard way, as our induction had not mentioned this rather crucial point, the emphasis having been mainly on the dangers of HIV/AIDS in the region.

It was a very lonely place for someone used to the bright lights and activity of London. The fear I had had before going to All Nations of ending up in some remote place, lonely and miserable, might actually be realised. Had I made a mistake? I had believed I was doing the right thing, that in spite of my rebellion, the God I had entrusted my life to many years earlier had guided me to this country. But sitting here in this isolated spot caused doubts to arise. After all the longing to live in Africa, was I to be disappointed? Could I trust the British Council, the Ministry of Education, or even my heavenly Father, to care for me in this remote and lonely place?

The school was built on a large, sandy plot and consisted of around ten modern, stand-alone, one-storey classrooms, an administration block and around 15 teachers' houses. A high perimeter wire fence surrounded the school. The houses were built alongside the fence at a slight distance from the school. Thanks to the Wednesday afternoon session of 'General Cleaning', during which all staff and pupils were responsible for mopping, washing and polishing the whole school, the entire complex and grounds were very clean and tidy. The surrounding dusty earth was likewise kept clear of weeds by regular sweeping using simple brooms made from dried twigs. This was assiduously attended to, not just to keep everything looking neat, but also to make sure snakes could not find a safe place to hide. A small guard's hut was positioned at the school gate, and this was used by the night-watchman whose job it was to patrol the school compound, guarding against thieves. It was well-known in Botswana that night-watchmen often fell asleep on the job – a fact which would come to light when a teacher's house or the classrooms had been burgled during the night.

Certainly, settling into Botswana presented me with many challenges, and the first year would prove to be a steep learning curve. Getting used to the unexpected was one of the first lessons. I encountered many frustrating situations in my early months of settling in, which were incredibly annoying at the time, but became subjects for much amusement afterwards.

Spiritually, Botswana was good for me. I felt my new life there was to be a fresh start in my relationship with my heavenly Father, which had turned rather sour over the previous five years. I prayed to be forgiven for my waywardness and reluctance to trust Him with every aspect of my life. The sense that I was forgiven was immediate, but for some reason I kept on asking for forgiveness over several weeks, perhaps out of a realisation at just how far away from Him I had wandered. Thankfully, the challenges and adjustments which I would face in Botswana provided many opportunities for me to depend on Him – opportunities I might not have had if I had remained in the UK.

I gradually settled into life at the school, enjoying my pupils, and grateful to meet Michelle, an art teacher from the Republic of Ireland who had also been placed at the school. Over the next two years we would spend many an hour chatting over mugs of tea about our experiences in Botswana. I also befriended a black and tan bitch called Cha Cha which belonged to another teacher. I took a liking to her and, knowing that dogs were not viewed by the Batswana in quite the same affectionate way as they are in the UK, I assumed her owner would be happy to sell her to me. However, he refused, so I turned to prayer, asking God to intervene but not really expecting Him to answer such a silly, insignificant and rather selfish request.

About a week later and, unsurprisingly, with no change of mind from Cha Cha's owner, I abandoned any thoughts of dog ownership. Keeping an animal could be inconvenient and, in any case, I didn't know how long I would be Botswana.

However, that was not the end of the story. One morning, returning to my bungalow at break-time, I saw something dark lying in the long dry grass on the other side of the perimeter fence at the back of my garden. Thinking it might be Cha Cha, I approached and peered through the wire. There, lying under a bush and sheltering from the intense sun, was a medium-sized black and tan dog, very similar to Cha Cha, only a bit smaller. Given the vastness of the area behind the fence, I wondered that the dog had lain down in this precise spot – just where I would see him.

I decided to walk round to take a closer look. In order to reach the dog I had to walk out of the school grounds. It was quite a circuitous route and I doubted the dog would still be there when I arrived.

To my surprise and delight, there he was. I approached cautiously, not wanting to frighten him away. Once I was near enough, I saw he was incredibly thin – literally a bag of bones. I also noticed that a thin metal wire had been tied round his left rear leg, there so long the skin had grown over the wire and the red, raw wound underneath. As an animal lover, I desperately wanted to help him but, fearful he might have rabies or some other disease, I was reluctant to simply pick him up and carry him home. After deliberating for a few moments, and knowing I was due back in class in about ten minutes, I decided there was nothing I could do. Thinking he would soon die anyway, I turned and walked sadly away.

However, as I made my way back through the long, dry grass, I was unable to get the dog out of my mind. So I quickly dropped by Michelle's house to tell her what I had seen. 'I want to do something but I've got a class in a few minutes,' I told her.

'Take the kids with you,' she replied, in a matter-of-fact way, seeing nothing unusual about the prospect of taking an entire class of children during school time on a dog rescue mission. This was Botswana, after all.

Accordingly, within around ten minutes I found myself marching out of the school grounds ahead of 30 excited children, myself armed with wire cutters, rubber gloves, a piece of rope and a fistful of dried dog food. Initially we couldn't find the injured dog anywhere. But then someone spotted him, still lying under a bush. I instructed the assembled group on how to rescue a dog. 'First, you go up to him gently and offer him some food,' I began, taking a couple of steps towards the dog, who was looking increasingly nervous of the crowd. I was within inches of reaching him, when suddenly, and to my dismay, he ran away. The children screamed with delight and gave chase.

Having seen what a terrible state the dog was in, his hip bones and ribs painfully sticking out, I was now desperate to help him, so I joined the children and together we belted across the dry terrain, the boys charging ahead while I followed with the girls, who were giggling helplessly at me, their white teacher, wearing rubber gloves and tight-fitting trousers, my long black cardigan flying in the wind.

With the boys in their white shirts by now just dots in the distance, I gave up the chase. It was no good. Then, within minutes of concluding it was a waste of time, one of the girls ran to me, panting, 'They hev got him, Medum. They hev got him.'

We reached the spot where a very tall boy, Kenanao, was holding the dog in a vice-like grip. I approached the terrified animal, quickly snipped off the length of wire, leaving the embedded part, and slipped the rope round his neck, after which we began the slow walk back to my bungalow, where I fed him and gave him water.

That night the dog slept on a makeshift bed of newspaper in the spare bedroom. I didn't sleep well, conscious of the fact I had a strange dog in my home, which might well be dead by morning.

Early the next day I cautiously opened the bedroom door and saw that the dog was still alive and had emptied his bowels on the tiled floor during the night. He got to his feet shakily and cowered, expecting a blow, as I approached him. Still feeling unsure, I gingerly put out my hand and lightly stroked the top of his head with my fingertips, at which point his tail wagged ever so slightly.

Mr Maseko, the headmaster, appeared baffled as to why I would go to so much trouble over an animal, but was nevertheless willing to lend me his 4x4 vehicle to transport the dog to a vet in Gaborone in exchange for posting some letters. As a result, the dog was tended to by a very kind South African vet who gave him a general anaesthetic before removing the embedded wire from his leg. He injected him against diseases and gave me some soothing antiseptic cream to put on the wound. He told me the dog was only around three years old. I then climbed back into the 4x4 and the vet gently placed the dog, still knocked out from the anaesthetic, onto the seat next to me. Surprised by the happy ending to this episode, I drove the long stretch back to Moshupa, the setting sun shining into my eyes and the dog's head resting on my lap.

Word about the rescue rapidly spread throughout the school and village. It would have been seen as a very unusual thing to do. But no one ever came to claim the dog. So he became mine and I named him Jake. He was the unexpected answer to my feeble, unbelieving prayer, a prayer that at the time I thought too unimportant for God to even listen to, let alone take seriously. I had expressed a wish, not really believing it would be met, and He had granted it in a completely unexpected way. It thrilled me to think that God took an interest in such apparently insignificant details of my life. Not only did I now have a gentle-natured dog to love and care for but, even better, I had experienced the loving intervention of my heavenly Father. Far away from everything that was familiar to me, I knew He was with me.

Of course, I needed a church to attend. Looking out across the brown, dusty village landscape of prickly trees, mud huts with thatched roofs and small, geometric, concrete buildings, it wasn't immediately obvious where I would find one. Unlike in the UK, where so many facilities are readily available and taken for granted, living in Botswana required me to be much more reliant on God. So I prayed that I would somehow find a church to go to.

About a week later I was returning home by bus after a grocery shopping trip in Gaborone. Night was drawing in as the Botswana sun began to rapidly melt into the horizon in a magnificent blaze of gold and red. The bus was old and rattled noisily as I, along with the local villagers, travelled through the darkening landscape. Then it happened. The engine cut out and the bus came to a grinding halt at the side of the road. Another bus wouldn't be along this way for at least an hour, we were told, so people started getting off. No one seemed surprised or particularly bothered –

except me. Picking up my plastic carrier bags full of groceries and sighing with frustration, I also disembarked.

I started walking, preferring to do that than hang around waiting for another bus which might not arrive. I found myself next to a slightly built man, about my height, who introduced himself as Josh from Zimbabwe and told me he lived in Thamaga, the next village before Moshupa. Having visited various non-European countries, mixed with people of many nationalities and lived in Brixton's multiracial community, I had become used to finding myself in cross-cultural situations and getting into the odd scrape or two. So I was happy enough to walk alongside Josh. I also knew that Botswana was, by and large, a very safe country, unlike South Africa, and I didn't feel threatened in any way.

As we walked along in the last vestiges of light, Josh mentioned that he was a Christian and described the Open Baptist Church he attended in Gaborone. Of course, I was eager to know more, wondering whether this might be the answer to my prayers for a church. Before we parted he wrote down the church's address for me.

My problem was that I lacked easy mobility without a vehicle. It was clear I would need to invest in a means of transport if I wanted to go to church in Gaborone, 60 kilometres away, and be generally more mobile. I didn't have enough money to buy a vehicle outright and, having heard that another British teacher had a Nissan pickup truck, known in the southern Africa region as a 'bakkie', for sale, I wondered whether this might be the answer. But how would I buy a truck without sufficient money?

Then I was introduced to Wilhelm, a teacher from Germany, with a view to asking him for a loan. In his mid-forties, he had been in Botswana for many years and had adopted the local way of life. When we talked about the possibility of a loan he told me he had been let down over repayments so many times he had discounted the practice. I came away disappointed.

That evening I picked up my Bible and read a verse I had often turned to from the book of Philippians: 'Do not be anxious about anything, but in every situation, by prayer and petition, with thanksgiving, present your requests to God' (Philippians 4:6). 'Easier said than done,' I thought as I climbed into bed. Feeling tired, I carelessly prayed about buying a vehicle before dropping off to sleep.

The next morning I was teaching a class when suddenly I noticed someone coming along the walkway next to the classroom. It was Wilhelm. Noticing that my attention was momentarily diverted, the children turned to look and, seeing a white man approaching, began making whooping and whistling sounds. I stepped outside to see what he wanted. 'I've had a think about it,' he began, 'and I'm happy to give you the loan – interest free.'

What an answer to prayer – and a feeble prayer at that! My heart soared as I realised God had unexpectedly provided for me again. As a result, I was soon in possession of the truck. With Jake happily perched on the cab seat next to me, we drove around the village dodging donkeys on the road, clouds of yellowish brown dust billowing skywards in our wake. Life had taken a real turn for the better. It was the first vehicle I had owned, bicycles aside. I now had the assurance that my heavenly Father was caring for me and fulfilling His promise to supply all my needs in my new country. Was He not worth following to the ends of the earth?

Chapter 19
A significant encounter

With some difficulty I managed to locate Open Baptist Church, tucked away in a small shopping mall in the capital. It was largely an expatriate church made up of several hundred people of many different nationalities from Africa, Europe, Asia and North America. I felt very much at home in this international community and looked forward to getting to know people.

On my second visit to the church, we were asked to greet someone sitting near us. I turned in my seat to see a couple who were a good deal older than me. I was 32 and they looked to be in their sixties. The man was tall and slim, with dark hair sprinkled with a little grey, a longish, angular face, clear blue eyes, thin lips and a trimmed moustache. His wife was short and petite, her mouse-coloured, shoulder-length hair atop a pleasant, kindly face, and no make-up.

We introduced ourselves and I was struck by how open and friendly they were. Their names were David and Ruth Gould. As I judged it, they weren't just being polite but were taking a genuine interest in me. Consequently, I found myself quite drawn to them. David was originally from England and was well spoken, but he rolled his Rs slightly and had a clipped South African twang. Ruth, of Danish extraction, was a farm girl from North Dakota in the USA, and there was no mistaking her accent. They were living in Pretoria, South Africa, and invited me to visit them sometime. South Africa had always been the main attraction for me, and since I had taken a liking to the Goulds, I decided I would take them up on their offer.

I planned sooner or later to make a trip to Pretoria to enrol for part-time History studies at the University of South Africa. So I decided to use the opportunity to visit the Goulds. As we were in Africa and they seemed to be genuinely hospitable, I assumed it would not be too remiss of me to simply turn up on the doorstep because, not having a phone, I had no way of letting them know beforehand.

When it came to the weekend of my intended visit, something happened which caused me to wonder at the significance of my earlier encounter with the Goulds. Michelle and I had taken Jake and Cha Cha for a walk. On the way back, the dogs were travelling in my open-backed truck, securely attached by leashes. As we drove through Moshupa, some schoolchildren pointed to the side of my truck. Being white in an African village, we were seen as objects of curiosity and had by now got used to people looking at us, sometimes calling out *'Lekgoa!'* (a racial slur descended from historical power relationships between blacks and whites) as we moved about the village. So, thinking nothing of it, I continued driving. But more children started pointing and shouting until finally Michelle stuck her head out of the window. 'Jake! Stop!' she shouted. I froze in my seat, slamming on the brakes. I was sure my beloved Jake must be wrapped round the wheel of the truck, dead.

In an instant Michelle and I leaped out of the cab. A crowd started to gather as I looked around for Jake. Where was he? One of the children pointed. There he was, limping towards the thatched huts, ears flat against his head, terrified. I sprinted after him and, frightened of what I might see, lifted him swiftly off his feet. The soft pads underneath were torn and bleeding. I realised Jake had, some minutes earlier, leaped out of the moving vehicle but, being tied, had had no option but to run alongside until he could run no more and had had to 'ski' on his feet.

There was no time to waste. Michelle and I bundled him into the back of the truck, his blood smearing against the base and sides. Squatting in the back, Michelle guarded Jake and Cha Cha while I slammed the cab door shut and sped off at breakneck speed, leaving the wide-eyed crowd standing in the middle of the road in a cloud of dust. If only we could get to the vet in time!

Arriving nearly one hour later, I saw to my dismay that the vet's was closed. I peered through the window and, in what appeared to be a miracle, saw him. To my great relief, Jake was soon bandaged, injected with a painkiller and looking a lot happier. His torn feet would heal.

Now there was no chance of travelling to South Africa for the weekend. Compared to what had happened to Jake, I realised my ruined plans weren't such a big deal, but I couldn't help feeling a bit disappointed, as I had been looking forward to meeting the Goulds again and now had to spend the weekend in Botswana instead of South Africa.

On Sunday I set off for church. After the service I got chatting with a British expatriate who, during our conversation, let me know that the Goulds were having lunch at her house. 'Join us if you want,' she added breezily, and gave me the address with directions. I was stunned. If it hadn't been for Jake's accident I would have driven to Pretoria and passed the Goulds coming in the opposite direction!

Initially I hadn't thought of my meeting this couple as especially significant. But I began to wonder. Had I again experienced God directing my life in unexpected ways?

I arrived at the lunch venue, a lovely, rambling, stone house which nestled on a hillside in Gabane village, a few miles west of Gaborone. The hillside was dotted with several houses belonging to expatriates, all uniquely designed, with attractive thatched roofs. I couldn't have imagined that one day I would live on this very hillside.

At the lunch I spent time talking with the Goulds. They told me they were planning to return to Botswana shortly – they had lived here some years before and owned two houses on the hillside. We assured each other that we would meet again. To them maybe I was just another young person among the myriad they had met in different countries. But I had a hunch this was going to be a significant friendship.

Chapter 20
Surrogate Dad

In 1997, not long after my arrival in southern Africa, David and Ruth returned to Botswana and, largely through the church, we became close friends. I paid regular visits to their rented house in Gaborone. It was a large, very attractive one-storey residence set in its own leafy, well-watered garden. Jake and I slept over on several occasions, avoiding the long journey back to Moshupa in the dark.

The house belonged to Dr Malcolm McArthur, founder and chairman of Flying Mission, an aviation missionary organisation in Botswana. Living next door was the grandson of Dr Robert Moffat, a well-known missionary to Bechuanaland (as Botswana was known in its days as a protectorate), whose daughter married David Livingstone, probably the best known missionary-explorer in history. Before long, whenever the Goulds travelled away for the weekend I found myself house-sitting at the McArthurs'. My time in Botswana was becoming a lot more interesting.

I had also begun History degree studies by correspondence with the University of South Africa. I had originally intended to study African History following on from the African Studies I undertook while living in Brixton, but the degree programme initially focused on

European history, something I knew very little about. In my spare time I found myself writing essays about the First and Second World Wars and thereby becoming fascinated by Adolf Hitler. I read tomes about his life while holidaying in Mozambique, much to the amusement of my travel companions.

Over the next two years, I spent a great deal of time with the Goulds, sharing meals with them and sometimes attending the Bible study they held in their next rented home in Phase 4, a district of Gaborone.

My two-year teaching contract was coming to an end but I was not ready to leave Botswana and certainly had no desire to return to the UK. In fact, I expected to spend the rest of my life in southern Africa, such was the grip the region exerted on my head and heart. It had become home, and I was hooked.

After completing my two-year contract in Moshupa and taking a short break in the UK, I was offered a three-year post at Molepolole College of Education, a government teacher training college in the village of Molepolole, 60 kilometres from the capital in a northerly direction. I was to teach trainee teachers, and part of my remit was to travel to various schools around the country and observe trainees on teaching practice. I much preferred this job to my previous one as it was more challenging and interesting. Visiting the schools invariably meant long drives, sometimes alone, across the vast Kalahari Desert region and would include overnight stays at motels in remote areas. Having a love of travel and adventure, I thoroughly enjoyed this aspect of the job.

But changing jobs meant I needed to move. I had had enough of village life in Moshupa and had no intention of moving to Molepolole which, although bigger than Moshupa, was still a long drive from the capital. The Goulds, aware of my predicament, invited me to become a lodger in their home. Like many houses in Gaborone, theirs was a single-storey, spacious dwelling, set in its own fenced-off compound. It was surrounded by a garden which contained succulent Kalahari species of plants and was a welcome green space in a semi-desert townscape.

Thus began our three years living together. Being in their sixties, the Goulds were twice my age, and they came to refer to me as their surrogate daughter, thereby implying that they were my surrogate parents. I was not the only 'adult child' the Goulds had taken under their wing over the years, notwithstanding their four natural children and a growing number of grandchildren. I was simply the latest in the surrogate series.

Most days I drove the 60 kilometres to and from work while Jake, my rescue dog, spent his time pottering around the hot, sunny garden, finding shady areas to lie down in. On my return I would pull up in front of the garden gate and Jake, hearing the loud rattling of the truck's diesel engine, would rush to the gate and leap high into the air over and over, such was his joy at seeing me. It was a wonderful welcome. I would often exercise him in the evenings when it was cooler, driving to a quiet place where I would follow dusty tracks and Jake would dart around, sniffing among the flora and rocks. I would climb onto one of the many boulders and sit with my arm around him to enjoy the arid, rocky scene, all the while keeping half an eye out for snakes and baboons which might attack him – or me.

David worked at his own accountancy firm, I. D. Gould and Associates, while Ruth, a retired nurse, ran the house, being hospitable to numerous guests and regularly visiting AIDS patients at the Princess Marina Hospital. While Ruth did most of the cooking, I usually did the washing-up. In the evening the three of us would sit together around the table, deep in conversation, covering a vast array of topics, often in the company of guests.

Unlike with Dad, I never had to second-guess David, my surrogate dad, since he spoke his mind, and no topics were off limits. It took some getting used to. I hadn't been accustomed to such open communication nor David's level of frankness. There was nothing quite like it, even among the choicest of my Christian friends. He and Ruth were so willing to lay bare practically any aspect of their lives, including details about their personal histories. Ruth had grown up in grinding poverty on a farm in North Dakota, while David had been raised in a relatively affluent business family in Essex. I was gradually able to piece their lives together, lives marked by unashamed Christian commitment.

I was particularly struck by the Goulds' honesty about their marriage. They never wore a mask of pretence that everything was wonderful. There was a transparency to them which I had not observed in other married couples. David spoke openly to me about their differences, admitting there were lots of problems in their marriage – but from my perspective their marriage appeared successful.

David didn't hold back from expressing his love for Ruth in front of me. One evening he asked her, 'Are you a tired little bear?' and then, gently stroking her fringe back, he said, 'I love you,' and I could see that he did. I had not witnessed such behaviour between my own parents and it felt odd, even a bit awkward, but at the same time I liked it. It was inclusive and open-handed and made me feel part of the Gould family. Though it was clear from their actions that people in my family did love each other, they never said so, and certainly not in front of non-family members.

After about a year, the Goulds decided to relocate to Gabane and live in their own hillside cottage. Jake and I were invited to go with them. Once there in my upstairs 'attic' room, complete with wooden beams and thatched roof, I had a view right across Gabane village to the capital 15 kilometres away. Every evening, as the crimson-gold sun sank beneath the horizon, the Gaborone lights would begin to twinkle, intensifying into a distant, sparkling lake of diamonds against the jet of night.

I had suspended a large mosquito net from a ceiling fan so that it covered the entire double bed I slept in. At night before getting into bed, I carefully tucked the edges of the net under the mattress. I had heard how a fellow expatriate on the hillside had been woken by a noise in the night, only to find that a scorpion had fallen from the thatched roof onto her pillow. Knowing that I was safely 'insulated' against creepy-crawlies meant I always got a good night's sleep.

The window at the back of my room looked on to the rocky hillside with its large boulders, interspersed by indigenous plant species. The hillside was a matter of metres from the window which I kept shut for fear of snakes and monkeys, if not baboons. Rumour had it that a leopard roamed the rugged terrain behind the cottage but, although I took Jake on many a walk there, I didn't see any wildlife except for birds, insects and the occasional scorpion. I grew to love the morning sound of cockerels crowing and the distinctive smell of distant rain as dark clouds gathered to unleash a torrential downpour. These storms would cause the dusty ground to release a wonderful aroma of wet earth, quite unlike anything I had smelled before.

Outside on the decking at night David, Ruth and I would look up and take in the night sky with its breathtaking myriad of stars. Seated here, absorbing the sounds of high-pitched crickets and watching the continual flashes of sheet lightning far away on the night horizon, we would continue to engage in lively discussions. The idea of spending our evenings slumped in front of a television was unthinkable. Television wasn't needed – and, in any case, was unavailable at the cottage. There was just too much to observe and consider in this fascinating environment to waste time on that. Our lives were full of extraordinary relationships with a diverse range of people and rich with a wonderful sense of community. This was, in Christian terms, 'abundant living' (see John 10:10). I had experienced this to a degree while living as a Christian in the UK but now, in Botswana, I felt I was living it more fully, and it was intoxicating.

I found my time living with the Goulds to be very healing. I had already experienced a measure of this through a number of healthy relationships since I had committed my life to Jesus, but this was healing at an altogether deeper level – a bit like radical heart surgery – and it was happening more than a decade since I had come to faith.

I observed that if my surrogate dad, David, had an opinion or belief about something, he would not simply talk it but would enact it. I noted that, in spite of his wealth, he and Ruth lived very modestly and had a strict view about the stewardship of money and possessions.

'People have no idea about the value of things,' he commented one day, having watched useful household items being thrown away. Given the consumerism and materialism of our age, this got me thinking. He and Ruth clearly did understand how valuable things are as I watched David try to repair their old top-loader washing machine for the umpteenth time. I knew they could easily have afforded a new one.

David, as a committed disciple of Jesus, seemed to have a firm grip on best practice for successful living. In spite of approaching their seventies, there was an innate drive and energy to the Goulds. They never lacked purpose or direction. I knew they had lived in many different places and had the impression they had always been very proactive, regardless of where they were living. 'We just get on with it wherever we are,' David told me one day.

As I saw it, there appeared to be no guile in David, and in the end I came to regard him as a person of great integrity. It was not as if there weren't any faults, of course. On the contrary, the Goulds had few qualms about telling me about their own weaknesses. Over time this level of honesty led to a depth of friendship that was rare for me.

However, I was still wary of giving too much away about myself. David, for example, had no idea that I aspired to have a family of my own.

All his offspring were married with children. I had often marvelled at how other people seemed to be able to find marriage partners relatively early in life, as David's children had done. In spite of the assurances from well-meaning Christians that I would eventually meet the right person, this had failed to happen. Now in my mid-thirties in Botswana, marriage seemed increasingly unlikely, so I never spoke about it. I later came to learn that this created the impression I was perfectly happy to be single.

I wanted to share my thoughts about marriage with the Goulds but reasoned, perhaps wrongly, that there was nothing they could do and that they might even counsel me to accept being single – something I didn't want to hear. It was 14 years since I had become a follower of Jesus and had started to want to have a family of my own, but the mystery as to why this had not happened remained unsolved.

In addition, I still wasn't very good at sharing my heart with people. I wanted to but still maintained the wall of independence and self-sufficiency I had erected as a young child living with my stepmother, Ella. At times my surrogate parents would giggle at my independence when, for example, instead of travelling with them in their car, I would drive my own vehicle to our common destination. On one occasion, David even got cross with me about this. Another time, while talking with him, I blurted out, 'I don't need anyone,' at which he was visibly shocked. Unhappy about my involuntary outburst, I wondered what had prompted it.

Years later, reflecting on our time in Botswana, David wrote from his home in Canada, 'You seemed very cautious at first to accept our invitation to be a lodger. I was not sure at the time – and not much clearer later, for that matter – why that was. You were reluctant to accept offers of assistance generally. Perhaps you thought that your independence was threatened. I never did solve that riddle, that puzzle. You were a single girl, a thoroughly single girl, as I read you, wanting to discover a way forward.'

Much of the time while living with them it simply didn't occur to me that I was being too independent. My childhood resolve to be self-sufficient in order to protect myself had become an ingrained mindset. It was my default position, a subconscious form of self-protection just in case something potentially threatening cropped up. It wasn't that I didn't trust anyone, but the independence I had experienced as a child, and which had served me so well thus far, wasn't something I wanted to let go of. Yet, now, as a Christian I was encouraged to increasingly learn dependence on God as Father, and to allow myself to rely more on other people as part of that.

Yet, whether I was aware of it or not, there was something I needed from my surrogate dad: acceptance. It was crucial for my journey towards wholeness, and in my friendship with the Goulds, particularly with David, that I felt accepted, something I had not experienced to any meaningful degree with Dad.

I benefited from the fact that David appeared to approve of me, as he supported and endorsed my decisions while offering his own perspective. He would affirm me with positive comments about my views and way of going about things. My History studies, which he showed an active interest in, had been going well before I moved in with the Goulds, but now things seemed to go up to another level altogether as I developed a passion for my subject and, with David's encouragement, went on self-planned history discovery trips to Berlin, Auschwitz in Poland, and Russia.

Enjoying David's approval, I didn't want to blow it. As with my primary school teacher Mr Land, and with Uncle David, it was important to me that I didn't do anything to undermine his apparent good opinion of me. I wanted him to think well of me so that I could continue to draw from him the nourishing sap of approval and affirmation he provided.

I learned that David had had his fair share of family relationship breakdowns, some of which had proved insoluble. So I was not alone in this and found I could apply his experiences with his siblings to my own situation with Dad. It was comforting to know I wasn't the only person living with a significant relationship which seemed permanently broken in spite of my best efforts to restore it. It helped lay to rest a lingering sense of guilt that I was the culprit in my story, and taught me that no matter how hard someone might try to fix a broken relationship, unless both parties were willing, reconciliation was impossible.

During those years with the Goulds I benefited from a surrogate fatherhood I had never known before. I wanted to learn from David as he lived by biblical principles and followed them consistently. In the end I realised he and Ruth had exerted more influence on me than anyone else in my life.

In 2002, as my time in Botswana was coming to an end and I prepared to depart for the UK, David said, 'This time in Botswana might well be something that you will look back on as significant.'

It was.

Chapter 21
Our distances apart

I was planning to return to the United Kingdom to study at the London School of Economics with a view to a change of job. I didn't want to leave southern Africa permanently and hoped to return, but the time had come for me to take a new path in life, even if it were only for a year.

One day, while sitting at the table, David, bracing himself slightly, turned to me and said he had been thinking about offering to pay a large chunk towards my tuition fees. This came as a complete surprise as I had intended to fund the entire study programme with money I had saved. Although I wasn't David's natural daughter, I felt that he treated me like one. I compared his offer with Dad's biannual £5 and his telling me he had earned every penny he owned and I had to do the same.

In due course I found myself back in London. I missed Botswana and my friends there terribly and cried whenever I thought about the happy community-focused life I had had there. I pined for the simplicity of life in southern Africa, the contact with nature, the quirkiness of the culture and the donkeys on the road. I struggled to adjust back to the very different, more independent way of living in the UK. I thought about how the Goulds simply got on with life wherever they were, and tried to apply it to my situation, but I found it very difficult. I ached for southern Africa and, in particular, for Botswana. I tried to drown my sorrows by often watching an amusing series of films based on fictional books set in Botswana. Deep down I felt that was where I belonged – and still do.

I put pen to paper to write to Dad, again via the law courts in Scarborough, informing him of my whereabouts. Sadly, as with all my attempts to re-establish contact with him over the previous 19 years, with the exception of one letter when I was 20, there was no reply.

During my last year in Botswana I had made a trip to Pretoria in South Africa to prepare for my History exams at the University of South Africa. On this visit, at the age of 36, I had met Alex, a South African born to an English mother and an Austrian father. Our paths had crossed at the home of an elderly South African lady called Margaret, where Alex was a lodger, and where I would temporarily stay while using the university library.

I felt when I met Alex that he ticked a number of the boxes on my mental list of qualities needful in a marriage partner. However, I also recognised that there were some very undesirable traits! Also, the most important 'box' of all – that of commitment to serving God no matter what – appeared to have a question mark hanging over it. Did he share my desire to spend my life telling people about Jesus?

In 2002, Alex packed up his life in South Africa and moved to the UK. We had already pretty much decided that we would probably get married, and his arrival in the UK was with the specific intent of going through with that.

However, when it came to it, the internal struggle I went through in deciding whether this was a right decision or not was nothing short of titanic and went on for many months. Friends, including the Goulds, had expressed misgivings about Alex as a choice for marriage. I had the added stress at the time of studying in the highly pressurised environment at the London School of Economics. I knew that marrying Alex would be the biggest risk I had ever taken. Yet when I looked back at the men I had met previously, how many of the available ones had come anywhere near what I was looking for?

Strangely, there were aspects of Dad which I saw in Alex, such as determination and a commitment to work. There was also the fact that both were balding, around the same height and build and wore glasses. But that was where the similarities ended.

In the end, in spite of my misgivings, and feeling somewhat stuck between a rock and a hard place, I decided to take the biggest risk of my life and began making plans for a wedding at St Helen's Bishopsgate in the City of London's Square Mile.

As these plans began to unfold, the question of who would give me away arose. I told myself it was probably pointless, but my first port of call was to ask Dad to do it, or at the very least to play the organ for us. Deciding I had nothing to lose, I asked Mum to approach him with my request. She wrote the letter and sent it through the law courts to be forwarded on; to where, we had no idea.

To our great surprise, a letter arrived from Dad. The postmark showed that it had been posted in Cannes, France – Dad's holiday destination, I surmised.

30th May 2003

Dear Ann,

Thank you for your letter of the 2nd May. Yes, I was surprised to receive it. However, I am pleased that Mandy is making a success of her life and is now to embark on matrimony and I wish her good luck for the future.

Sadly I will not be able to play the organ at the wedding since I suffer from stiffness in my fingers and have had to curtail my activities in that area.

I do not wish to rake over past history concerning our lives but I am unable to participate due also to our distances apart.

Finally it would be nice to hear from Andrew. If you are in contact please suggest writing to me through the law courts in Scarborough.

I will forward some money to defray expenses through the usual court offices.

Ken.

It was not clear to me quite what he meant by 'distances apart'. Was he referring to the geographical distance or emotional distance? In the end I went with the latter, given that it had been preceded by a reference to what had happened in our lives in the past. Indeed, when I stopped to analyse it, the distance between us had always been there; it had simply grown wider as the years had gone by.

I was very surprised by Dad's offer of money towards the wedding, and for a moment I entertained the idea that it could be the start of a more open attitude, but when I enquired as to how much it was, Mum told me it was the compulsory maintenance payments due to her, paid months in advance – around £100.

My heart sank. It dawned on me that if he wasn't prepared to make the effort to attend his own daughter's wedding, or to make a meaningful contribution, that signalled this was a hopeless case. Why had I even bothered, I asked myself, just to be let down all over again?

The next most obvious person to give me away was my surrogate dad, David Gould. He and Ruth were still living in Botswana, so covering the distance to make it to my wedding would entail quite a commitment. Thinking back over the time we had spent together in Botswana I felt reasonably confident that he would be willing. However, the answer was 'no', and David remained silent as to the reasons why he was unwilling to give me away.

In the end, Uncle David agreed to do it. 'Is he a nice uncle?' David Gould had enquired, concerned that I should at least be given away by someone I liked. Of that there was no question, the only fly in the ointment now being that Uncle David and I had never agreed about the Christian faith, which was central to my life. Yet he graciously agreed to give me away and make a 'father's' speech at the reception.

On an occasion some years later David Gould observed, 'If you were my natural daughter I would have done it.' Now came the rub. Of course, I reminded myself, I couldn't really expect to be treated in quite the same way as a *natural* daughter. It was fair enough, I reasoned, but it taught me one thing: there were limits even to the best of earthly fatherhood, be it surrogate, adopted or even natural. Clearly, for me at any rate, a perfect earthly father was not someone I was ever going to meet; nor should I expect to.

Chapter 22
Surprised by love

The people who had known me the longest would never have described me as maternal. Throughout my young adulthood I had no interest in children. I dreaded going to houses where there were toddlers or primary school-aged children as I didn't know how to interact with them. Beyond regular but brief visits to Uncle David, I had little experience of young children, being far more drawn to animals. Animals were straightforward and didn't change. People, on the other hand, could be selfish and unpredictable.

And yet I knew that one day I wanted a family of my own, a family unlike my childhood one, a family where both parents would be present and any children would grow up in a secure, loving environment, encouraged to reach their potential. Yet I had no idea what sort of parent I would make. The student I had dated at All Nations had told me I wouldn't make a good mother because of my childhood experiences and, on one occasion, while giggling with Joanna at my lack of maternal instinct, she had said, 'You'd make a terrible mum!'

Three months into our marriage I discovered I was pregnant. I was ready to embark on a new experience in life and curious to discover what the big fuss about children was; only I didn't feel especially maternal towards the little being I was now carrying. Unlike some mothers-to-be, I didn't revel in pregnancy or stroke my growing bump as I had often seen other women do. Instead I felt quite trapped, knowing that big changes to my body were taking place and I wasn't in control of any of them. Dramatised portrayals of childbirth on television and personal scare-stories of motherhood didn't help either.

I was also concerned that I might become mother to a girl. Throughout my adult years I had always preferred male company to female – something else which may have had its root in my childhood experiences with my stepmother. This might well have accounted for my preferences when it came to what sex my own child would be. Of course, I had no control over this. I expressed my concern to a female friend, that I wasn't sure I would be able to love my child if it were a girl.

'No, I can assure you,' she told me, 'even if you do have a girl you'll love her just as much as you would a boy.' But was she right?

In addition to this, as terrible as it sounds, I didn't really see the life I was carrying as a person, perhaps because I had absolutely no experience of children. Although I was more or less happy to be pregnant, I couldn't help having mixed feelings. I really couldn't be bothered with all the fuss of antenatal classes and didn't want to end up surrounded by women who talked about nothing but babies. As a result, I knew practically nothing about what to expect when it came to the actual birth.

Also, at the back of my mind, I was afraid of losing my freedom, which had always been very important to me. To counteract this, and probably against my better judgement, six weeks before my due date I booked a flight to Botswana. 'That's cutting it a bit fine, isn't it?' my long-time friend Joanna had commented.

'It's a last-ditch attempt at freedom,' I laughingly explained to people who raised their eyebrows when I told them about my travel plans. Yet, in truth, it wasn't a joke. I really didn't want to lose my freedom and independence.

I simply carried on with my travel plans almost as if the baby weren't there, arriving first in South Africa after an 11-hour flight and staying with friends. Then, as I would normally do, I borrowed a car and drove the five-hour stretch to Botswana alone on isolated roads.

I had arranged to stay with Marion in Botswana. She was a British expatriate who had lived in Africa for many years and had offered to take care of Jake in my absence. She now lived in a large, self-built wooden bungalow on a large plot of land in an isolated spot called Phakalane, several miles outside of the capital.

As soon as I arrived and pulled up outside her bungalow, Jake appeared. I opened the car door and immediately he remembered me, his tail wagging so furiously that the whole of his back end wagged with it. Later that evening, as he was not allowed to sit on the sofas, he sat at a slight distance, his eyes, like dark pools, fixed on me. I wanted to hold him and never let him go. It thrilled my heart to see him but also broke it that I knew I would soon have to leave and perhaps never see him alive again. He was now ten years old. I took him for one of our walks to some nearby swamps and on short car journeys to visit friends, and sat with him in Marion's garden, watching him contentedly licking his paws. It was just like old times.

The nearest neighbour was Marion's son who lived in a large two-storey house on the same plot, but in the event of an emergency, even he was far enough away not to hear a call for help. Marion became concerned that all the bouncing around in her truck as we drove along the rugged dust roads would cause me to go into labour. It was something I hadn't even considered when planning my trip to Botswana. The fact that this could be a potentially perilous situation for a pregnant woman to be in didn't enter my mind, such was my thrill at being back in Botswana.

Alarmingly, I had a frightening episode of hypoglycaemia, low blood sugar, while staying with Marion, in which my vision became severely disturbed. Neither of us knew what was happening until Marion gave me something to eat, after which my vision returned to normal. Needless to say, this landed me at the doctor's, where I was chastised for travelling to Botswana so close to my due date.

Reflecting on this now, it does strike me that my behaviour was a bit reckless, but the explanation was quite simple, and it surfaced one afternoon when Marion and I were having coffee in a shopping mall in Gaborone. We were discussing the fact that I was pregnant and how my life was about to change from bordering on Bohemian to somewhat more conventional. I then passed a comment, referring to the baby as an 'it'.

Looking slightly shocked, Marion said, 'That's your baby you're talking about.'

I looked at her, surprised by the unexpected rebuke. What had seemed like an ordinary comment to me had clearly struck her as unusual. When I later reflected on this, it made me realise that even at this late stage of events I didn't appear to have particularly strong maternal feelings towards the little life I was carrying. It seemed to indicate I was almost in denial of this reality. I began to wonder again what sort of parent I would make. Would I even *like* this baby? After all, I wasn't really interested in other people's babies; why should I be interested in my own? I can only speculate that my experiences as a child – separation, neglect and rejection – were shaping my responses as I stood on the cusp of parenthood.

My time in Botswana had come to an end. I opened the boot of the car to put my small case into it. But as soon as I did so, Jake sprang inside the boot and settled himself down for the journey. He seemed to be saying, 'I'm coming with you.' He would not obey my instruction to get out, and it was the hardest thing for me to pull him out. I didn't want to be parted from him. I wanted to stay, to resume my life here in the place I had come to love: Botswana. But I had no choice and was soon on my way, the car bouncing erratically on the long dirt track that led from Marion's house to the main tarred road. I glanced in the rear-view mirror at the clouds of yellowish-brown dust billowing upwards in my wake. But the view was obscured by a flood of tears which wouldn't stop. All I could think about was the life I had had in Botswana, and Jake. Would I ever see him again?

My return journey to the UK passed without mishap, but then I found myself frequenting King's College Hospital in London. My blood pressure had gone up quite significantly and the doctors thought I might be in danger of pre-eclampsia, a dangerous condition associated with the late stages of pregnancy. The risk was clearly too much for one consultant who, on one of my routine check-ups, ordered me to be admitted immediately to a ward so the baby could be induced. Frightened by the suddenness of this and the fact that within a few hours I might be holding a baby, or that something terrible might happen to me, my first instinct was to turn and run.

Then, as I sat in the consultation room, faced with the reality of the new life I was carrying, an unexpected determination arose in me at the eleventh hour. I now became very concerned that my baby should have the best possible birth. The process of induction failed and, refusing to be induced a second time or have a Caesarean, I signed a disclaimer and discharged myself from hospital. I believed that my baby should be born in the natural way unless it was clearly a matter of life and death.

A week later saw the onset of a natural birth. During the process, which lasted 50 hours, I went through a terrible time, the pain rendering me unable to eat or sleep throughout. Alex supplied me with one bucketful of iced water after another. For some reason I had an insatiable craving for it, pouring it down my throat in huge gulps as if my life depended on it. I then vomited some of it back up several times over. I was in so much long and drawn-out pain that in the end all I wanted was to be free of the baby.

Such was the agony that at one point I felt I almost didn't care what happened as long as the pain would stop.

Once the baby was born I lay on the bed in total shock and exhaustion. All I knew at this stage was that I now had a baby boy. All my fears about having a girl had been unfounded.

'Would you like to hold your baby?' came the nurse's voice.

'No, not yet,' I replied as I lay taking in the fact that I was no longer in excruciating agony. 'Is it normal for me to not want to instantly hold my baby?' I wondered.

From my bed I looked to the left and watched as our close friend Margaret, Alex's former landlady, who was visiting from South Africa, held my newborn baby – I was quite happy for her to do so. Then the baby was brought over to me. I propped myself up in the bed and put out my arms to receive him. The nurse placed him gently in my arms, and for the first time I was able to look at him properly.

Then it happened. Within a split second of looking down into his misty, unseeing little eyes, I was completely and utterly smitten. Seemingly from nowhere I experienced a tremendous wave of overwhelming love for this tiny, helpless person. It was greater than any love I had ever known.

In an instant my non-maternal perspective changed. As I cradled him I knew that right now what mattered most to me was his welfare. I knew straightaway that I wanted to be the very best I could for him. He was depending completely on me, and I didn't want to let him down. I wanted to make sure I didn't do anything that would ruin his chances in life. I wanted him to have the very best I could give, to know how utterly loved he was, how totally wanted and infinitely precious – and all this in the space of a few minutes of making eye contact with him.

We named him Tristan. The bond he and I developed over the coming weeks was so strong I couldn't bear to be parted from him, even for ten minutes. Thinking that I had been in our flat too long – around ten days without going out – Alex insisted on taking me for a short drive in the car, leaving Tristan in the care of a visiting friend. But as we drove round the nearby streets of Peckham, tears began to form in my eyes. I didn't want to be away from my precious Tristan even for one minute.

From the day of his birth, Tristan became the all-consuming focus of my life. Many decisions would be made on his behalf, and both Alex and I were committed to making the right ones. Likewise, the birth 14 months later of another boy, Zack, resulted in an equally powerful bond forming between us. Zack made the family complete.

As a new father, Alex too had a strong emotional response. He would sometimes burst into tears when announcing Tristan's arrival to family and friends over the phone. While attending Zack's birth, his first reaction was to take off his shirt and hold Zack's tiny, pink body to his chest. I would not have described Alex as especially interested in children prior to having his own, but once the boys were born he became a committed dad.

We read one or two books about the parenting of boys and how they, more than girls, need to bond with an ongoing parent figure in the first three years of life, and that key to a boy's development is the fact that he would need to latch on to his father at around the age of seven. We took these things very seriously and made our decisions based on what we understood to be the boys' primary needs.

This reading backed up my instinct that Tristan and Zack needed to be with me every day of their young lives. I looked back to the way Mum had denied herself a social life and opportunities to go out and work as she had done previously in order to provide a continuous parental presence at home. She was there when I left for school and when I came back, providing meals and constantly encouraging me to study hard. Her commitment, in spite of all the difficulties, now helped me to seek to do the same for my own children. There was now no possibility in my mind of looking for a full-time job, even after a year or two. I knew my work was right here, with my two boys.

As the years went by, hardly a day passed without the boys being told, 'I love you; you are so precious, special and unique.' I didn't want them ever to face trauma similar to that which Andrew and I had gone through. I wanted to make sure I had no regrets when it came to my boys. Perhaps that was expecting too much, because the challenges of marriage and parenting are sometimes profound. But the one thing that spurred me on was the desire to see them grow into happy, well-rounded adults who have a sense of identity, destiny and purpose in God. As a parent, I knew this was worth giving everything for.

Chapter 23
Reflections

It was at the significant time of Tristan's birth that I decided once again to try to establish contact with Dad. This time it was through a friend who had access to records from which she was able to trace him to Eastbourne – even down to the road and house number!

With a baby just a few months old, I contemplated a surprise visit to Dad. As the weeks went by I gave this a lot of thought, but every time I did so the fear that I would be turned away on the doorstep became very real. Which would be worse: seeing Dad and being sent packing, or living with the possibility of never seeing him again? I dithered for several weeks then decided that I should first test the waters by sending a short letter and a photograph of Tristan to the Eastbourne address. Surely the sight of his grandson would move him to act.

I wrote the letter, slotted in a photo of Tristan and posted it off. I waited. Several days went by without any response. The days became weeks, then months. I did the same after Zack's birth 11 months later. Then, to my shock, the envelope containing the letter and photo of Zack were returned. It had been opened then taped closed again and sent back with the words 'Gone Away' written on the front.

Was it Dad's way of shaking me off the trail, or had he really moved away – again? And what had happened to the first letter and photo of Tristan?

Sometime after this a chance encounter between Mum and two Christians who lived in Eastbourne led to the couple visiting Dad's address and finding out from the neighbours that he had moved away to Lincoln 'to be near family'. The only family that could possibly be was Ella's son, who by now might have children of his own – children who perhaps would refer to *my* Dad as 'Grandad'.

The trail had gone cold.

My last attempt to re-establish contact was made through the Salvation Army Family Tracing Service. The service was available to people who wanted to make contact with close relatives with whom they had lost touch. As such I qualified to apply, and, having paid the nominal fee and supplied them with the necessary details, I waited.

It was sometime later that a letter arrived from the Salvation Army stating that their search for him had yielded results, but as Dad had not responded positively to their communication they were unable to take the matter any further. They were not permitted to disclose any addresses – indeed, such was the privacy surrounding these searches that it was not the Salvation Army themselves who carried them out but an undisclosed third party.

There now appeared to be no sensible options open to me. I had exhausted all avenues; all internet search engines had drawn a blank, even the electoral roll. Family tracing websites are sufficient to reveal that he is still alive as this book goes to print, but beyond that, in spite of the efforts of more than 30 years, I have been unable to make any progress towards reconciliation.

Some have said it is perhaps in my best interests never to see Dad again, justifying this by recounting a story of someone who wished they hadn't found their long-lost dad, the reunion being traumatic. Others have sometimes told me how their estranged dad reappeared in their lives – and the same could happen to me.

It would be misguided to claim that my relationship with my heavenly Father now supplants all need for an earthly father. The role of a father figure, whether natural, adoptive or surrogate, is indispensable and far-reaching, and the benefits that result from good fatherhood cannot be underestimated.

In 2010 something happened which confirmed this to me. It was on a June morning, when my family and I were all peacefully sleeping, that the phone rang at 6.30am. Alex answered. After listening for a few moments he blurted out, 'What?' His loud voice resonated through my ears. I knew instantly that something terrible had happened, and swallowed hard.

'Uncle David's gone,' Alex said.

My uncle, my teenage father figure and role model, had collapsed and died while taking an evening stroll along the beach the previous evening. The shock was seismic. I lay in bed staring in disbelief at the ceiling. I couldn't take it in. Later, however, my incredulity at the news made me appreciate just how important he had been to me. Even though we never could agree about Jesus Christ, Uncle David had been a very influential person in my life. As a result, I have found it hard to come to terms with this loss.

Today, six years later, I often have to pinch myself and ask, 'Did that *really* happen?'

Through these experiences of an earthly father, father figures and surrogate fatherhood, the main lesson had to be that there could only be one perfect father: God. I have experienced His fatherhood over many years, in spite of my own weaknesses, waywardness, doubts and poor decisions.

Yet I have struggled with what appears to be unanswered prayer for my brother, that he would make some semblance of a recovery and decide to follow Jesus too. 'Why did I come to faith but my brother hasn't?' I once asked a Christian friend.

'I don't know,' came her honest reply.

Then there were the many prayers for Uncle David, that he would come to realise that Jesus Christ is Lord; and for Dad, that he would have a change of heart and take up my offer of a reconciliation. These things did not and still have not happened, and I have no answers as to why. I draw comfort from the fact that even David Gould, my surrogate dad, whose life appears to have been, and still is, richly blessed by God, didn't have all his dreams come true concerning broken relationships in his own family.

Recently I was sitting with a disabled Christian friend who, many years ago, was rejected by his entire family and lost contact with them all. He was, as far as family was concerned, alone in the world.

'Don't you ever think of looking for your relatives?' I asked him.

'No,' he replied, without hesitation. 'I've got Father God.'

Of course, I told myself, if he could find God sufficient for his needs, then so could I. As I have discovered, part of His all-sufficient care is that He can provide an earthly, 'surrogate' father for those who need one. I have experienced the truth of the words, 'God sets the lonely in families' (Psalm 68:6). He set me in the Gould family as a surrogate daughter and now, following David and Ruth's example, I have enjoyed the blessing over a number of years of including our disabled friend in my family, where he has become our sons' fun-loving and generous surrogate uncle.

I have learned that my heavenly Father pays attention to the smallest detail – 'Not one [sparrow] will fall to the ground outside your Father's care,' said Jesus (Matthew 10:29). This is the awesomeness of God, Who leads me to the truth, Who guides, protects and provides for me in spite of myself and no matter where I go – even to the ends of the earth. He 'is the same yesterday and today and for ever' (Hebrews 13:8).

In 2007 Alex, the boys and I were due to visit Botswana. Sadly, one week before the flight, Marion called to tell me Jake had died. I cried over the phone as she broke the news to me. He usually slept outside and came into the bungalow in the morning for his food. But on that particular day he had not appeared. A short search around the compound revealed that he had lain down and died of old age during the night. He was around 13 years old.

On arriving at Marion's house, the first thing I did was to go and look at the place where he was buried. I stood, staring down at the small mound under a low-growing prickly bush – not dissimilar to the one under which I had found him ten years previously. My precious Jake was no more. In 2002, when I had left Botswana, I had thought I would return to live in southern Africa once I had completed my studies in London. I had not known at the time of my departure that I would never live with Jake again.

I often thought about him, and it was only in 2013 that I felt ready to own another dog, one that Tristan and Zack would benefit from taking care of. So we visited the world-renowned Battersea Dogs' & Cats' Home in London, but we didn't immediately see a dog we thought was suitable. I wanted to get the right dog for our family and, since the Bible encourages us to 'pray about everything' (Philippians 4:6, NLT) we asked God to choose a dog for us. I had learned that even though this was a small matter when viewed against the seriousness of global affairs, it wasn't too small for my heavenly Father, my Dad, any more than it would have been for an earthly father.

Two weeks went by as we continued to look at the various dogs on offer. Then we decided to wait because we really wanted the dog that God had chosen for us. Alex had a preference for stocky Staffordshire bull terriers, whereas I preferred more slender breeds. How would we ever find a dog we could agree on?

Within a few days the phone rang. A litter of six puppies had been brought into the home and all had been rehomed except for one. Young puppies were always snapped up quickly and, as we had been waiting a week or so, the people at the home asked whether we would like them to reserve the puppy for us.

We eagerly agreed and arranged to go and meet our new 'family member'. Sitting in a room waiting for the puppy to be brought to us, we had little idea about what it looked like, not even the colour: our only information was that it was a Staffordshire-cross bitch and would grow into a medium-sized dog. We weren't entirely sure what we were getting, but since we had prayed and waited, we believed this dog was God's choice.

The door opened and a member of staff walked in holding a tiny female pup – a Staffordshire bull terrier crossed with a whippet, we were told. I chuckled at this comical coupling. 'She hasn't had a good start to life,' the assistant informed us, and pointed to some small scars on the puppy's head. The small pup gambolled playfully around the room, chewing on a piece of rope and furiously wagging her spindly tail. Delighted to have a dog of their own, the boys fell on her, eager to pick her up while she licked them and tried to chew their hands.

And as I looked down at her, I had to smile. She was black and tan.

God will wipe away every tear from their eyes.
(Revelation 7:17)

Prayer

If you have been impacted by this story and would like to commit your life to Jesus today, you might like to pray the following prayer:

Dear heavenly Father,

Thank You for all that You have done for me through the cross. I believe that Jesus is the Son of God, and that He paid the price for all my wrongdoing when He suffered there. I believe He died and rose from the dead.

Forgive me for all the things I have said and done which have hurt You and other people. I accept Jesus as my Lord and Saviour. I am turning away from my wrongdoing.

Please fill me with your Holy Spirit so I can live for you from this moment onwards.

Thank You, Father.

Amen.